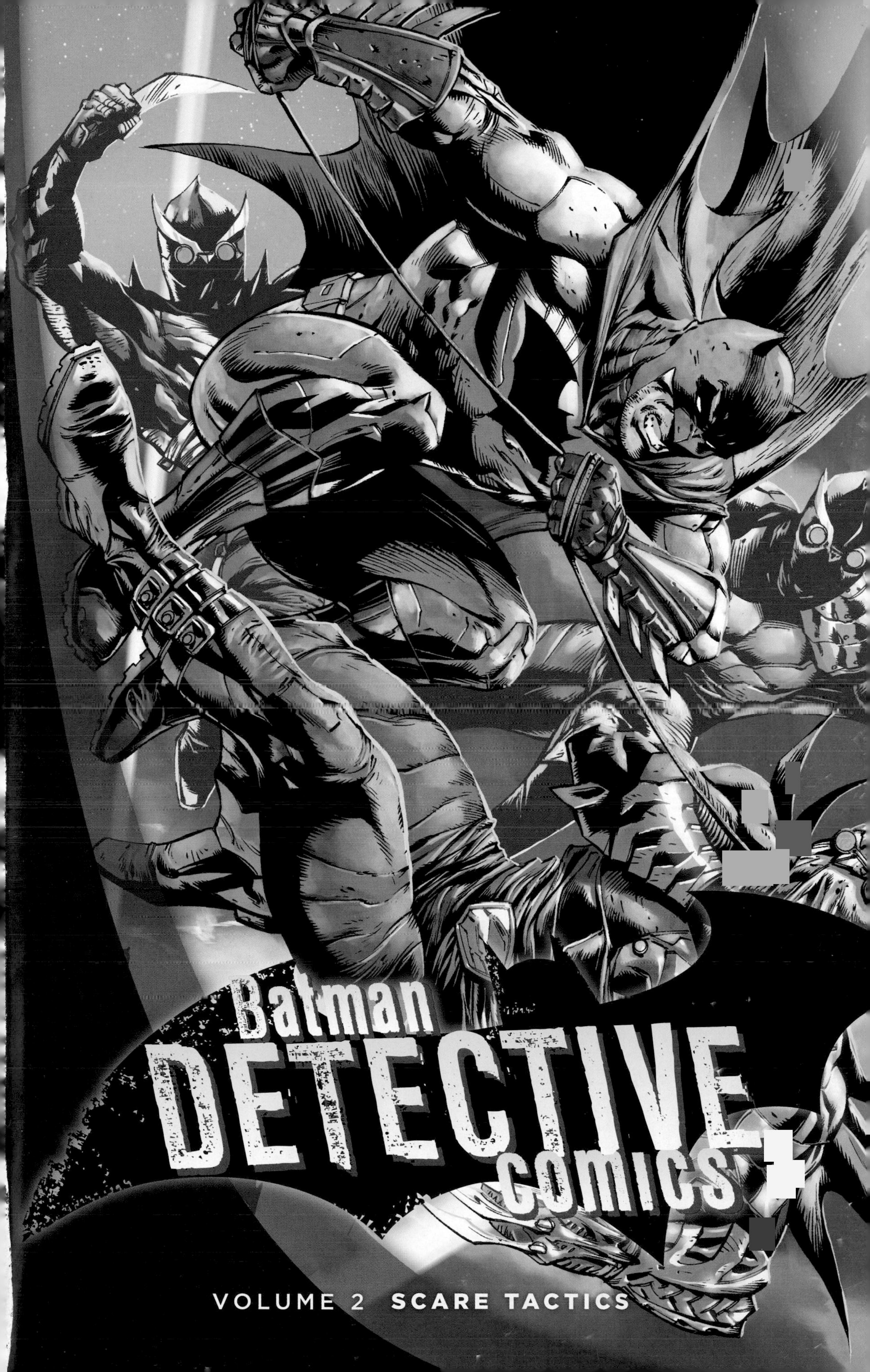
Batman
DETECTIVE
COMICS
VOLUME 2 SCARE TACTICS

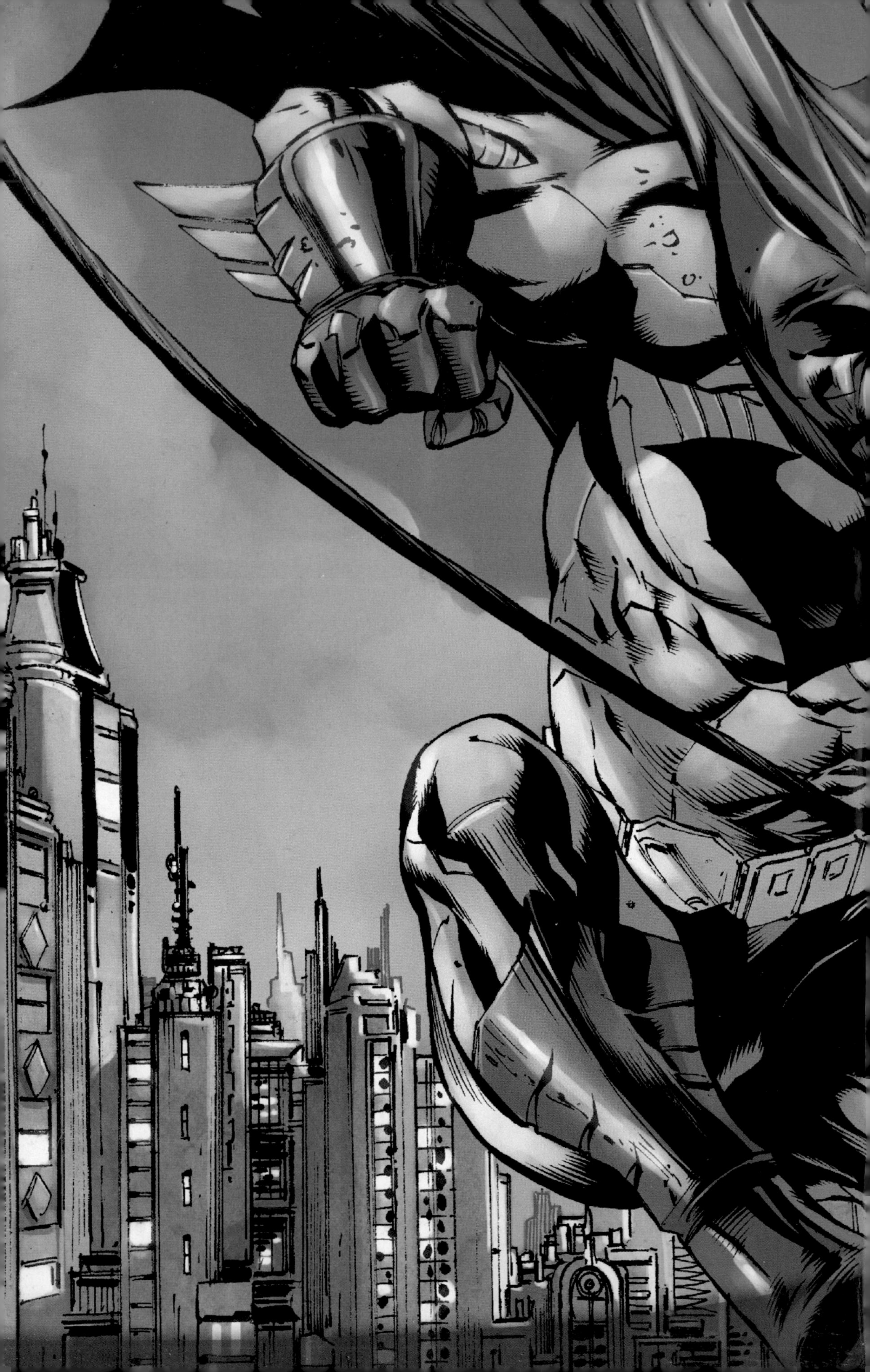

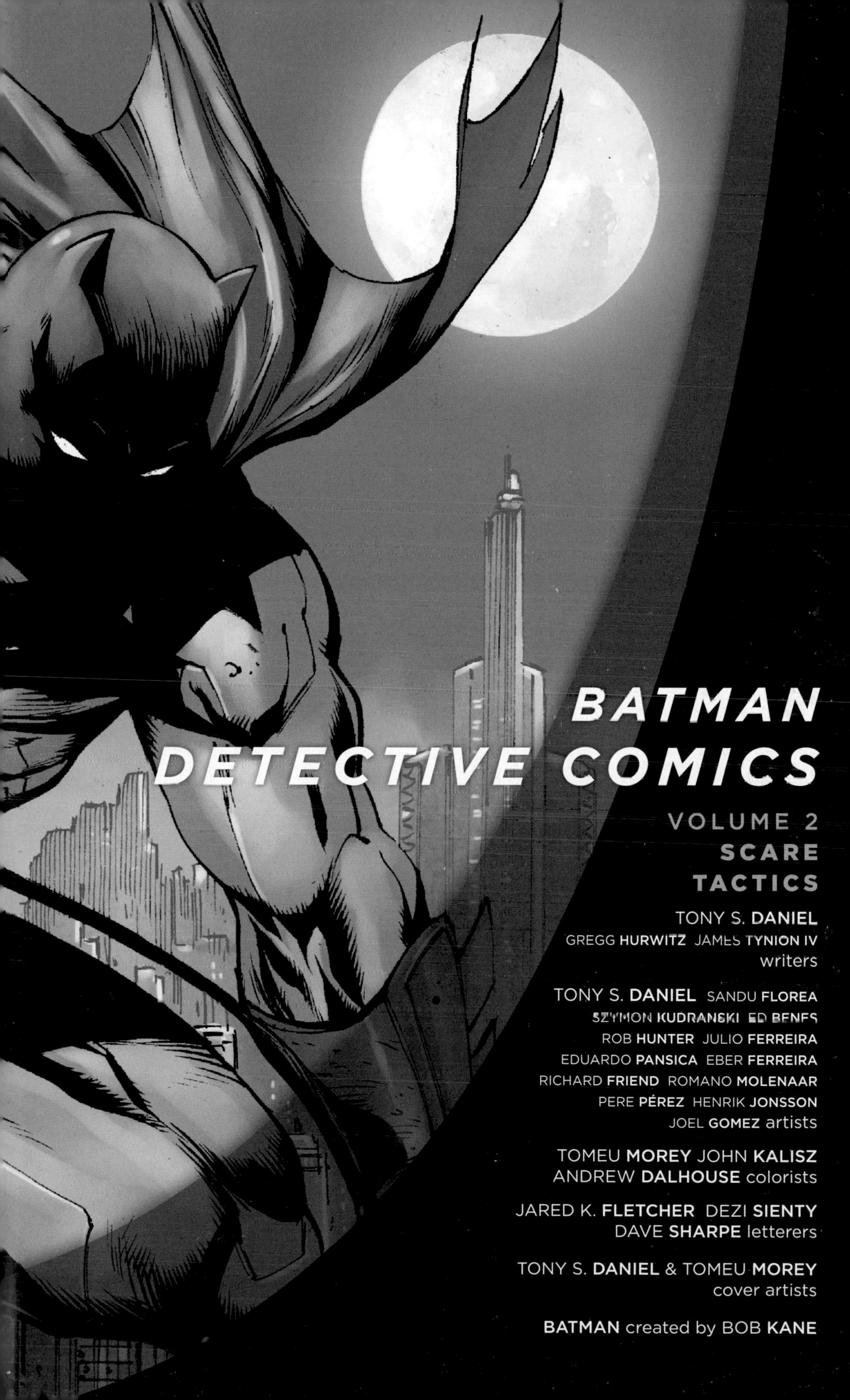

BATMAN DETECTIVE COMICS

VOLUME 2
SCARE TACTICS

TONY S. **DANIEL**
GREGG **HURWITZ** JAMES **TYNION IV**
writers

TONY S. **DANIEL** SANDU **FLOREA**
SZYMON **KUDRANSKI** ED **BENES**
ROB **HUNTER** JULIO **FERREIRA**
EDUARDO **PANSICA** EBER **FERREIRA**
RICHARD **FRIEND** ROMANO **MOLENAAR**
PERE **PÉREZ** HENRIK **JONSSON**
JOEL **GOMEZ** artists

TOMEU **MOREY** JOHN **KALISZ**
ANDREW **DALHOUSE** colorists

JARED K. **FLETCHER** DEZI **SIENTY**
DAVE **SHARPE** letterers

TONY S. **DANIEL** & TOMEU **MOREY**
cover artists

BATMAN created by BOB **KANE**

MIKE MARTS Editor - Original Series HARVEY RICHARDS Associate Editor - Original Series
KATIE KUBERT Assistant Editor - Original Series PETER HAMBOUSSI Editor
ROBBIN BROSTERMAN Design Director - Books ROBBIE BIEDERMAN Publication Design

BOB HARRAS VP - Editor-in-Chief

DIANE NELSON President DAN DIDIO and JIM LEE Co-Publishers
GEOFF JOHNS Chief Creative Officer
JOHN ROOD Executive VP - Sales, Marketing and Business Development
AMY GENKINS Senior VP - Business and Legal Affairs NAIRI GARDINER Senior VP - Finance
JEFF BOISON VP - Publishing Operations MARK CHIARELLO VP - Art Direction and Design
JOHN CUNNINGHAM VP - Marketing TERRI CUNNINGHAM VP - Talent Relations and Services
ALISON GILL Senior VP - Manufacturing and Operations HANK KANALZ Senior VP - Digital
JAY KOGAN VP - Business and Legal Affairs, Publishing JACK MAHAN VP - Business Affairs, Talent
NICK NAPOLITANO VP - Manufacturing Administration SUE POHJA VP - Book Sales
COURTNEY SIMMONS Senior VP - Publicity BOB WAYNE Senior VP - Sales

BATMAN - DETECTIVE COMICS VOLUME 2: SCARE TACTICS

DC Comics, 1700 Broadway, New York, NY 10019
A Warner Bros. Entertainment Company.
Printed by RR Donnelley, Salem, VA, USA. 3/1/13. First Printing.

HC ISBN: 978-1-4012-3840-7
SC ISBN: 978-1-4012-4265-7

SUSTAINABLE FORESTRY INITIATIVE
Certified Chain of Custody
At Least 20% Certified Forest Content
www.sfiprogram.org
SFI-01042
APPLIES TO TEXT STOCK ONLY

Library of Congress Cataloging-in-Publication Data

Daniel, Tony S. (Antonio Salvador)
Batman Detective Comics. Volume 2, Scare Tactics / Tony S. Daniel.
pages cm
"Originally published in single magazine form in Batman: Detective Comics 0, 8-12, Detective Comics Annual 1."
ISBN 978-1-4012-3840-7
1. Graphic novels. I. Title. II. Title: Scare Tactics.
PN6728.B36D355 2013
741.5'973—dc23
2012046018

Carson City

Library

Date: 9/5/2017

Time: 3:14:53 PM

Total Checked Out: 2

Checked Out

Title: Batman-Detective Comics. Volume 7, Anarky
Barcode: 31472400252528
Due Date: 10/03/2017 23:59:59

itle: Batman Detective Comics. Volume 2, Scar
ics
31472400154567
10/03/2017 23:59:59

GOTHAM CITY'S DISEASE CONTROL LABORATORIES...
Batman in DETECTIVE COMICS
SCARE TACTICS
Written and pencilled by TONY S. DANIEL
Inks by SANDU FLOREA
background assists by JOEL GOMEZ
colors by TOMEU MOREY
lettering by JARED K. FLETCHER
cover by TONY S. DANIEL and TOMEU MOREY
The woman falling to her death is Selina Kyle, A.K.A. Catwoman.
To Gotham's police force, she's a costumed cat burglar.
To Gotham's people, the occasional vigilante.
And to me, Gotham's Dark Knight, she an on-again, off-again...dancing partner.
CRASH
She'd been hired by some mystery man to break into Gotham's Hazard Materials lab and s something of value
What that something is isn't important to me.

10:45 P.M.
She's not herself right now.
Her mind is a scramble of fear and panic.
Or worse.
CATWOMAN, STOP!
YOU?! IT'S REALLY YOU?!

DON'T TRUST YOUR EYES. YOUR MIND'S PLAYING *TRICKS!*
YOU WANT TO *KILL* ME, *POISON IVY?*
AND HERE I THOUGHT YOU *BIRDS OF PREY* PLAYED ON THE SIDE OF THE ANGELS...
RELAX--
--I CAN HELP YOU.
GAAAHHH!
LOOK INTO MY *EYES.*

LOOK AT ME, DAMMIT!
She's been poisoned by Scarecrow's fear gas.
PSHHP
Fortunately for her, I have the antidote.
STAY A-WAAAAYYYY...
She'll have one hell of a hangover, but I only have forty-five minutes left.

FIFTEEN MINUTES AGO. 10:30 P.M.
GOTHAM CITY POLICE HEADQUARTERS.
WHAT DOES SCARECROW WANT, COMMISSIONER?
CAN'T BE SURE EXACTLY. I FOUND THE PHONE ON MY DESK ABOUT AN HOUR AGO.
HE MADE IT VERY CLEAR THAT HARM WOULD COME TO SOMEONE IF I DIDN'T PUT HIM IN CONTACT WITH YOU.
HE HAS A HOSTAGE?
THAT'S THE IMPRESSION HE GAVE. BUT FOR ALL WE KNOW--
BREEP BREEP
IT'S HIM.
Scarecrow runs down the rules of his game.
Either I play, or his captive will suffer.
ONE HOUR, BATMAN. ENOUGH TIME FOR YOU TO COMPLETE THREE EASY ERRANDS FOR ME.
IF YOU LEAVE NOW, YOU CAN GET STARTED WITH THE FIRST: FIND CATWOMAN'S PAWS IN THE COOKIE JAR ON THE NINETEENTH FLOOR OF THE DISEASE CONTROL LABS.
SECOND, DEDUCE WHO SHE WAS GOING TO RENDEZVOUS WITH AND WHERE.
LASTLY, FIND THEM.

"SHE WAS HIRED TO SNATCH SOMETHING VERY DEAR TO ME.
"SPECIMENS OF THE ANTI-FEAR AGENT YOU DEVELOPED FOR THE POLICE TO USE AGAINST ME AFTER OUR RECENT TUSSLE ON HARMON ISLAND.
"IN THE WRONG HANDS, WELL--I'D HATE TO THINK OF HOW FAR I'D HAVE TO GO TO PUT THINGS BACK IN ORDER."
HUFF HUFF
WHERE WERE YOU TAKING THE ANTI-FEAR TOXIN CAPSULES, CATWOMAN?
B-BATMAN? I- UHN ...MY SPLITTIN' HEAD...
YOU WERE EXPOSED TO SCARECROW'S FEAR GAS.
BUT I HAVEN'T BEEN ANYWHERE NEAR THAT CREEP...
...I... I'VE BEEN MANIPULATED BY THAT--
"BY THAT" WHO?
WAIT A MINUTE! I CAN'T THINK STRAIGHT!
TRY HARDER! WHAT'S THE LAST THING THAT WAS CLEAR TO YOU? NAMES, FACES-- THINK!

10:51 P.M.
I hate to leave her that way, but things have been... **tense** between us lately.
The mission takes Priority and I got what I needed.
The name: **Digger Jones.**
The place: the old newspaper plant on Printer's Row.
I know the location. And if there's business going on inside

--it won't be good.
GET HIM, BOY!
RARRG
GRAARL
TEAR HIS FACE OFF!
LOOKIT HIM!
HE GOT HIM! HE GOT HIM!
BAM
SHOW'S OVER.
ANYONE GOT A PROBLEM WITH THAT?
HOLY--
IT'S THE BAT!
DIGGER JONES. NOW!

HUFF HUFF HUFF HUFF
Digger Jones--low level drug-dealing, armed robbery, and now dog-fighting.
His trajectory will eventually lead him back to me.
I-I GOT A GUN, MAN! THIS IS SELF-DEFENSE, YOU KNOW?
BRAKASH
Whether he likes it or not.
WHERE WERE YOU HAVING CATWOMAN TAKE THE ANTI-FEAR PILLS?! WHERE?!

11:05 P.M.
RAFF RAFF RAFF RAFF RAFF RAFF
LOOKS LIKE YOUR DOGS ARE MALNOURISHED, DIGGER. HOPE THEY DON'T CONFUSE *YOU* FOR THIS *PORTER-HOUSE.*
OKAY, *OKAY!* I-I WAS GONNA MEET THESE GUYS WITH SOME OF MY BEST DOGS.
THEY... THEY WERE GONNA *EXPERIMENT.*
WHERE?
GRRRLL
GRRRLL
THE BUILDING AT THE END OF DEARBORN STREET. THE OLD PRIVATE SCHOOL.
BREEP BREEP

WELL DONE, BATMAN! WE MAKE A **GREAT TEAM,** DON'TCHA THINK?
BREEP BREEP
I'VE PLAYED YOUR GAME, SCARECROW. NOW TELL ME ABOUT YOUR HOSTAGE.
IN DUE TIME. YOU HAVE ***ONE MORE CHALLENGE*** TO EARN THAT RIGHT.
NOW LEAVE THE ANIMAL ABUSER TO THE POLICE AND GET HOPPING.
THAT'S A BIG MISSTEP, SCARECROW. NOW I KNOW YOU'RE WATCHING ME.
Run, Scarecrow.
Run fast.

FOR YOUR SAKE, I HOPE THERE ISN'T ANY REAL HOSTAGE. THAT THIS IS JUST PART OF YOUR GAME.
I NEVER TOLD GORDON THERE WAS A HOSTAGE. BUT THERE IS A VICTIM, BATMAN. ISN'T THERE ALWAYS?
THE GAME YOU'RE PLAYING WITH ME WILL INDEED SAVE SOMEONE'S LIFE. BUT FIRST YOU MUST HANDLE ONE LAST BIT OF BUSINESS.
GET TO THAT OLD SCHOOL. DESTROY EVERYTHING AND EVERYONE THERE! UNDERSTAND?
SOMEONE ELSE HAS STOLEN YOUR RECIPE FOR HELL ON EARTH AND YOU'RE UPSET ABOUT IT.
I GET IT.
OH, PLEASE. YOU GET TO SAVE SOMEONE FROM THE ABYSS. AND I CAN DESTROY MY ENEMY. IT'S A WIN-WIN.

IF THE END RESULT IS YOU BEING FREE TO TERRORIZE GOTHAM, THEN IT'S A LOSE-LOSE.
SOK
YOU IDIOT!
SOK
PSSSHHHHHH
THE WAY I SEE IT, I HAVE ALL I NEED TO STOP YOUR ENEMIES AND PUT YOU AWAY.
YOU'LL SCREW UP EVERYTHING!
NO. I'M GOING TO FIX THIS.
BAMF
SKTCHH
TIME'S SLIPPING AWAY, BATMAN--

--JUST AS THE VICTIM IS SLIPPING THROUGH YOUR FINGERS!
YOU'LL FIND HIM THERE, AT THE DEARBORN ADDRESS.
"THE BOY CAN BE SAVED ONLY IF YOU STOP THEIR OPERATION.
"IF YOU FAIL... YOU FAIL HIM."
THE GAME IS OVER, SCARECROW.
11:26 P.M.
1510 DEARBORN STREET.
I leave Scarecrow bound to the chimney and tip off Gordon.
I know I'll get there first.

I wouldn't have it any other way.
There are at least a dozen Scarecrow impostors along the school's perimeter.
TH-WINK
Whatever they're up to, it looks like more than a dress rehearsal.

I have to play it safe for the sake of the boy.
PSSSHHHHHH
At least until the element of surprise is gone.
WHAM
Then I can break some faces and get to the core of the situation.
WHAP
And I will.

SOMEWHERE INSIDE...
GRAB SOME OF THOSE GUARDS TO LOAD UP THE VANS.
WE NEED TO GET THESE BOXES OUT OF HERE *BEFORE* MY FATHER ARRIVES.
ELI, YOUR FATHER'S ON SATELLITE. HE WANTS TO SPEAK WITH YOU. RIGHT NOW.
FINE. THAT WORKS BETTER FOR EVERYONE.
DAD, I'M HAPPY TO SEE YOU TRUST ME ENOUGH TO OVERSEE--
SHUT UP, ELI. MY SOURCE TELLS ME THE POLICE ARE EN ROUTE TO YOUR LOCATION.
DROP WHAT YOU HAVE AND GET OUT *IMMEDIATELY.*
BUT THE CHEMICALS. I MEAN, AM I SUPPOSED TO JUST *LEAVE* THEM HERE?
YOU'RE LUCKY I HAVE CONNECTIONS. I SHOULD JUST LET YOU ROT IN JAIL FOR--
SHK!
WHA--?

BATMAN?! SOMEBODY SHOOT HIM FOR CRYIN' OUT--
FORGET IT.
SNAP
AHHH!
SMACK
NOW. WHERE'S THE KID?
I'M GOING TO COUNT TO *ZERO* BEFORE I SNAP YOUR NECK LIKE I DID YOUR WRIST.

W-WHAT KID? I-I--
HE'S *HERE.* I *KNOW* HE IS. I KNOW...
...YOU...
...YOU.
HE'S *YOU.*

11:31 P.M.
The young man going by the name Eli Strange claims to be the son of Professor Hugo Strange, a noted Gotham scientist with an extensive criminal record.
His birth records show his name as Elliot Montrose. Born to a Julia Montrose who died in the delivery room.
GO
PO
No father was listed on the birth certificate.
Adopted by middle-class parents, it was soon realized by the time he was four that Elliot was gifted.
By age ten he graduated from college.
By age seventeen he was working at the Pentagon. He used his talents to help decode sensitive foreign diplomat communications.
Both of his supervisors died in separate freak accidents two weeks apart. A month later, he turns up here in Gotham.
Scarecrow was wrong about Elliot Strange being a victim.
The intended victim was Gotham City. Mass-produced fear toxins were intended to be used by unknown entities for unknown reasons.
Catastrophe was averted.
At least for one more night.

Florea

TONY DANIEL
-12-
Florea

NIGHT OF THE OWLS, 8:26 PM...
ARKHAM ISLAND.
IS HE GONNA LOWER THAT DAMN BRIDGE OR WHAT?
BEEEEP
BEEEEP
THE ISLAND'S ON LOCKDOWN, SIR.
I'M SUPPOSED TO TELL YOU BOYS TO WAIT HERE TILL WE GET THE "ALL CLEAR."
ON WHOSE ORDERS?
COMMISSIONER GORDON'S.
LOOKS LIKE WE'RE JUST EXTRA BODIES, THEN.
HAVE YOU BEEN DRINKING TONIGHT, KID?
ME, SIR? N-NO. I HAVEN'T.
THEN HAVE A SEAT.

THEY SAY IT'S GONNA BE A *LONG NIGHT.*
HEY, YOU GOT HEAT IN THERE? BEEN FREEZING MY TOES OFF IN THAT MEAT LOCKER EVER SINCE THEY CUT BACK ON THE GAS BILL...
HOO HOO-OOO
HA, GOOD MAN! MIGHT AS WELL MAKE FRIENDS. HOW LONG YOU S'POSE WE'RE GONNA BE WAITING?
DON'T KNOW, DON'T CA--
THE HELL?
BOOMPF
WHATEVER BOUNCED OFF YOUR HOOD WAS *HEAVY.*
MAYBE A LOONY GOT OUT. BUT IF THAT'S THE CASE, HE'S PLAYING GAMES WITH THE WRONG MAN...
POLICE

Batman in
DETECTIVE Comics
NIGHT OF THE OWLS
THE OWLS TAKE ARKHAM
I see no "clear and present danger" tonight.
Written and pencilled by TONY S. DANIEL
Inks by SANDU FLOREA
colors by TOMEU MOREY
lettering by JARED K. FLETCHER
cover by TONY S. DANIEL, SANDU FLOREA and TOMEU MOREY

Surely, not more than any other night.
This is the safest place in Gotham City.
Mind you, the Asylum has the greatest security measures in the United States--
--dare I say, the world.
I'M PROUD OF YOUR PROGRESS, MR. ZSASZ. KEEP IT UP.
I'M ALWAYS UP, DR. ARKHAM. HAVE NO DOUBT.
For the patients here, my Asylum is a safe haven from the improper treatment dispensed inside the cells of Blackgate Prison--
--as well as a haven from themselves.
At Arkham, my guests can mend their minds at a natural pace (albeit with a little help from highly specialized treatment programs).
There is no better place on Earth for them.
Or me.
THE POLICE SUGGEST WE SECURE OURSELVES INSIDE THE SAFE ROOM UNTIL THEY HAVE ENOUGH MAN-POWER TO ESCORT YOU OUT.
A.CASH
NONSENSE, MR. CASH. THIS ENTIRE STRUCTURE IS OUR SAFE ROOM.
WITH ALL DUE RESPECT, DOCTOR--YOUR NAME TURNED UP ON A HIT LIST.
ACCORDING TO THE G.C.P.D., ANY NUMBER OF HIGHLY TRAINED ASSASSINS ARE ON THEIR WAY TO THE ASYLUM RIGHT NOW. WE DON'T KNOW WHO THEY ARE OR WHY THEY'RE COMING, BUT...
...WE CANNOT TAKE ANY CHANCES.
OUR ISLAND IS ON LOCKDOWN. NO ONE CAN GET IN OR OUT.
LET GOTHAM SORT OUT ITS TROUBLES OUT THERE. IN HERE, WE ARE ALL SAFE...
...PLUS, I HAVE WORK TO DO BEFORE LIGHTS OUT. MY PATIENTS ARE COUNTING ON ME.

Like Patient 372, A.K.A. Steeljacket.
Genetically manipulated, his bones are as hollow as his mind. He is a victim--as are the others I've come to know so well in recent months.
Like Linda Friitawa, or Fright.
Victimized by both Scarecrow and the Penguin. Disfigured inside and out by illegal chemicals fused with her blood cells during so-called "medical studies."
Then there's Basil Karlo, known infamously as Clayface.
Victimized and betrayed by his own lust for fame. A tragic set of events turned him into what he has now become...
...an untouchable behemoth with an outer malleable membrane instead of flesh.
Or take Nocturna, for example. Why, just the other day, she--
DR. ARKHAM, IT'S ROMAN SIONIS. HE'S READY TO END HIS HUNGER STRIKE--BUT HE WANTS TO TALK TO YOU FIRST.

Yes, being strapped down and force-fed intravenously will do that to a man.
Roman Sionis, A.K.A. the **Black Mask.** He's quite a...**unique** patient.
Thought dead just two years ago, he turned himself in, begging to be cured of his...**affliction.**
I welcomed him in and have been battling with the court system ever since.
He'll soon stand trial for his role in leading the gang known as the **False Face Society**, but only after I deem him fit to stand trial--
--a scenario that seems farther away with each passing day.
DOCTOR, I'VE COME TO MY GOOD SENSES, YOU'LL BE HAPPY TO HEAR.
I WANT TO **LIVE.** I WANT TO **BE WELL!**
THAT'S A WONDERFUL FIRST STEP, ROMAN.
BUT I CAN'T DO IT ALONE. I NEED **HELP** FROM MY--
NOW, NOW. LET'S NOT START--
DOCTOR, YOU'VE AVOIDED ME EVER SINCE...
...WELL, SINCE YOU TOOK MY **PARTNER** AWAY...FOR THAT **JOYRIDE.**
I CAN ASSURE YOU, THE RIDE WAS **ANYTHING** BUT JOYFUL, ROMAN.
IN FACT, IT TAUGHT ME HOW DANGEROUS AND DESTRUCTIVE YOUR PARTNER CAN BE.

YOU TWO MUST NEVER BE REUNITED. YOUR PARTNER NOT ONLY CONTROLS YOU, BUT ANYONE YOU--
THOOOM
WHAT?
LIGHTS OUT EARLY TONIGHT--EH, DOCTOR? BUT WE'RE NOT DONE TALKING--
A STORM MUST BE APPROACHING. THE BACKUP GENERATOR WILL KICK IN S--
The flicker in his eyes--designates movement.
Behind me!
ZHHZCHT
GUHRN!
JEREMIAH ARKHAM, FOR HARBORING AND ENCOURAGING CRIMINALS, THE COURT OF OWLS HAS SENTENCED YOU...
...TO DIE.
THERE IS NO USE DELAYING THE INEVITABLE.
OUR WORK CAN BE SWIFT, JEREMIAH.
OR NEEDLESSLY PROLONGED. THE CHOICE IS YOURS.
BAM

NIGHT OF THE OWLS, 8:51 PM...
BOOM
BOOM

RUN!
RUN LIKE HELL, ARKHAM!
BOOM
MY FREEZE GRENADES WILL SLOW THE TALONS DOWN. I CAN ONLY HOLD THEM BACK FOR SO LONG!
MOVE IT, DOCTOR!
BOOM
Batman! I should have guessed...he must have led these fiends to my sanctuary!

Got to get away. Mustn't get swept up.
I KNOW THE ASYLUM HAS SEVERAL HIDDEN POINTS OF ESCAPE, DOCTOR.
CHOOSE ONE AND GET THERE!
CRUNCH
NOW!
BAM
CHAACK
UGHN!
BATMAN, YOU CANNOT STOP THE COURT OF OWLS FROM REACHING ITS TARGET...
...FROM KILLING ARKHAM!

Anyone deranged enough to invade my Asylum is welcome to stay and be analyzed by my staff.
Batman, particularly.
Who knows? Perhaps I could...fix him.
WHAT HIDDEN ESCAPES DOES HE MEAN, DOCTOR?
JUST GIBBERISH, MR. CASH.
ARKHAM
DOCTOR ARKHAM, YOU HAVE JUST EARNED A SLOW DEATH.
SMACK
GO!
I'm fleeing inside my own sanctuary. My home.
B-DEEP DEEP
I must fix this at any cost!
CLAMP
ARGH!
Roman Sionis. Yes. He's my only hope.

My home has been invaded for the sole purpose of destroying me--
--destroying everything that I and my ancestors have made here.
Brilliant men like Amadeus Arkham.
TONIGHT, YOUR SAFE HAVEN HAS UNINVITED GUESTS.
ONES WHO, IF NOT STOPPED, WILL DESTROY EVERYTHING YOU'VE COME TO RELY ON FOR YOUR SAFETY, ROMAN SIONIS...
"...I WILL HAVE TO TRUST THE EVIL I KNOW MORE THAN THE EVIL I DON'T..."

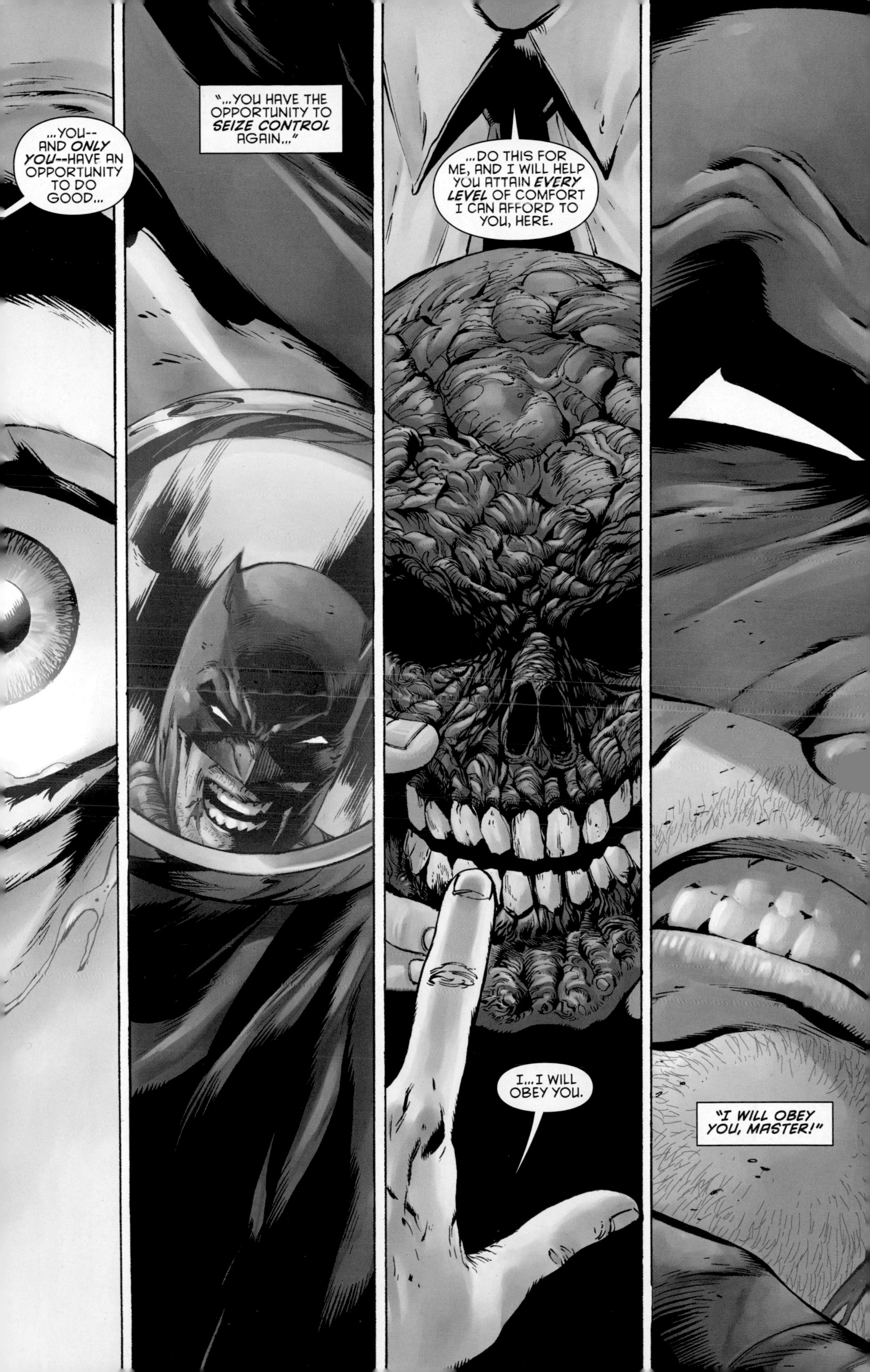
...YOU--
AND *ONLY YOU*--HAVE AN OPPORTUNITY TO DO GOOD...
"...YOU HAVE THE OPPORTUNITY TO *SEIZE CONTROL* AGAIN..."
...DO THIS FOR ME, AND I WILL HELP YOU ATTAIN *EVERY LEVEL* OF COMFORT I CAN AFFORD TO YOU, HERE.
I...I WILL OBEY YOU.
"I WILL OBEY YOU, MASTER!"

He's crushing my throat. Can't get out from this Talon's grasp!
YOUR VOCAL CORDS WILL BE RUPTURED. HOW HORRIBLE.
-GRGHH!-
I WANT TO HEAR YOU BEG FOR YOUR LIFE.
CRAK
WHAT IS THIS? A TRICK?
VMBK-MMMMMMMMM
The cell behind me...opening!
BRASHH
I CAN'T HELP MYSELF, PUNKS! I HAVE AN INCREDIBLE URGE TO COMPLETELY RIP YOU TWO APART!
Clayface?

AND BY THE LOOKS OF IT, I'D SAY I'M NOT ALONE IN THAT THOUGHT.
WE ARE SURROUNDED.
THEY'RE STILL NO MATCH FOR US.
The inmates are free. But their focus is on the Talons.
By all rights, they should be pouncing on me as well.
But they're not.
107103
10224
Arkham Asylum is highly compartmentalized. One chamber seals into another.
B-DEEP DEEP
They can fight it out in the cell block until Gordon can afford the manpower to regain control.

WELL DONE, DARK KNIGHT.
WE CAN NOW SORT OUT OUR BUSINESS-- UNDISTURBED FROM THAT CHAOS OUT THERE.
BLACK MASK? IS THAT YOU, ROMAN?
ROMAN SIONIS IS MY MASK, BATMAN.
WHAT ARE YOU...DOING TO MY HEAD?
JUST SUGGESTING YOUR NEXT COURSE OF ACTION, BATMAN.
DR. ARKHAM TOLD ME TO STOP THE INTRUDERS. AND YOU ARE AN INTRUDER.
BLAME HIM FOR TH--
GAAAAAAAH!
YOUR POWERS PREY ON THE WEAK MINDED.
CHUK
DO I LOOK WEAK TO YOU?
N-NO!
ARKHAM. WHERE IS HE?

Complete and utter chaos!
Sector Seven is under the influence of Black Mask's mind control, and the patients still can't take down those assassins!
Batman did a brilliant job containing them for me.
Now all I have to do is wait for the **sleeping gas** to overcome them and--
BOOM
What is--
BOOM BOOM
Right outside my door! One of them has followed me somehow!
BOOM BOOM BOOM
BOOM BOOM BOOM
BOOOM

CRASH
BATMAN? Y-YOU?!
ROMAN SIONIS HAS BEEN PUT BACK IN HIS CAGE. NO NEED TO THANK ME, ARKHAM.
SIONIS WAS FREE? HOW--
SHUT IT. YOU'RE COMING WITH ME.
YOU'RE INSANE! YOU CAN'T--
BAP
RELAX, DOCTOR. IT'LL BE A SHORT RIDE.

WHUP WHUP WHUP
WHUP WHUP WHUP
LOOKS LIKE BACKUP'S FINALLY ARRIVED.
AND THE POWER'S BACK ON, TOO. I'LL LOWER THE BRIDGE SO YOU CAN GET DR. ARKHAM OUT OF THERE. WE HAVE THE OKAY FROM GORDON.
POLICE
YOU HEAR THAT?
HEAR WHAT?
VROOOOOMMMMMMM
HEH.

NIGHT OF THE OWLS, 9:49 PM...
GRN... WH-WHAT'S... GOING...
BATMAN, I'VE BEEN TRYING TO REACH YOU--EVERYTHING OKAY? WILLIAM COBB AND I--
THERE'S NOT ENOUGH TIME IN THIS ONE NIGHT, NIGHTWING...
BEEE-DEEET
...I HAVE DR. ARKHAM WITH ME NOW. HE'S ALIVE. I NEED TO GET HIM SOMEPLACE SAFE IN A HURRY.
BAP
EVERYONE'S ANSWERING YOUR CALL, BUT I CAN TAKE ARKHAM OFF YOUR HANDS. JUST TELL ME WHERE TO MEET YOU.
I'LL DUMP HIM OFF ON MY WAY.
I NEED TO FIND THE BIRDS OF PREY...AND TRACK DOWN LINCOLN MARCH, NOW.
This long night has gotten longer...

GOTHAM CITY'S BUSINESS DISTRICT...
YOU'D THINK THEY WOULD'A PICKED A BETTER TIME OF DAY TO TRANSPORT THIS CARGO. TRAFFIC'S NUTS.
GOTHAM CITY TRUST
BEEEEP
SCREEEEE
WHOAH! WHAT'S THIS JERK DOING?
HEY, STAN... LOOKS LIKE THEY'RE GETTING OUT...?
THIS DON'T LOOK GOOD...
MOVE IT, MIKE!
WE GOTTA PROTECT WHAT'S IN BACK!
BOOOOM
WHAT THE--

BOOOM
MIKE, YOU OKAY?
STAN, LOOK, IT'S BAT--
OH, YOU GOTTA BE KIDDING ME...
Batman in DETECTIVE comics
ON THE BRINK
Written by TONY S. DANIEL
Pencilled by ED BENES
Inks by ROB HUNTER
colors by TOMEU MOREY
lettering by JARED K. FLETCHER
cover by DANIEL and MOREY

TH-THAT ISN'T BATMAN, MIKE!
GO! GO NOW!

YOU KNOW OUR ORDERS, STAN.
SHOOT TO KILL. YOU DON'T HAVE TO TELL ME TWICE!
BLAM
BLAM BLAM
BRAKAKA BRAKAKA BRAKAKA BRAKA
MOVE QUICKLY. WE ONLY HAVE A FEW MINUTES.
OPEN THE BACK OF THE TRUCK.
LET'S FINISH THE JOB.

ACROSS TOWN...
GOTHAM
GOTHAM MEMORIAL HOSPITAL
I'M SORRY, SIR...
...BUT YOU'RE NOT ALLOWED IN HERE. THE PATIENT REQUESTS--
NO, MAGGIE. IT'S OKAY. I'D LIKE TO SEE MR. WAYNE.
SORRY, I DON'T MEAN TO BE SO *PERSISTENT,* CHARLOTTE. BUT YOU KNOW...I--
I'M THE ONE WHO'S SORRY, BRUCE. I JUST HAVEN'T...
...IT'S HARD FOR ME TO BE AROUND ANYONE RIGHT NOW. MY SURGERIES HAVE KEPT ME WELL-SEDATED, AND--
YOU DON'T HAVE TO EXPLAIN ANYTHING TO ME. I UNDERSTAND.
HERE...I BROUGHT BEAUTIFUL FLOWERS FOR A BEAUTIFUL WOMAN.
YOU SAY THAT NOW--
UHHH BUT I'M THE *BRIDE OF FRANKENSTEIN* UNDER THIS ROBE.

NONSENSE.
IS THAT WHAT YOU'RE AFRAID OF--?
BRUCE... NO.
THEN... WHAT IS IT, CHARLOTTE?
I... I JUST NEED TIME TO HEAL. TO FIGURE THINGS OUT FOR MYSELF.
I... I'M ACTUALLY MOVING TO PARIS. THERE'S A GREAT OPPORTUNITY THAT'S OPENED UP--
PARIS?
I CAN'T TURN THIS DOWN, BRUCE.
I CAN'T STAY PUT. YOU KNOW ME.
DON'T YOU?
RIGHT, YOU NEED TO GET AWAY. I UNDERSTAND... IT'S NATURAL TO NEED SPACE.
BOOM BOOM
I NEED TIME TO THINK, TOO. BUT... PARIS?

IT'S FAR... THE ADJUSTMENT WILL BE DIFFICULT. BUT IT'S WHAT I NEED.
IT'LL KEEP MY MIND BUSY ON SOMETHING OTHER THAN...MY SISTER. SOMETHING OTHER THAN JILL.
I SHOULD'VE DONE MORE TO HELP HER OUT. I GUESS I'M FEELING GUILTY FOR BEING SO SELF-ABSORBED THESE LAST FEW YEARS.
YOU KNOW?
BRUCE?
BOOM BOOM BOOM
BOOM BOOM
YES. I UNDERSTAND. YOU NEED TO GET AWAY.
ARE YOU EVEN LISTENING TO ME?
CHARLOTTE, I HAVE TO--
BRUCE, JUST TELL ME YOU UNDERSTAND. PLEASE--SAY IT?
BRUCE, YOU KNOW HOW I FEEL...YOU KNOW--
BOOM BOOM BOOM
YES. I DO.
BOOM
More than you know.

THIS IS GORDON! I NEED EVERY MAN AVAILABLE--NOW, DAMMIT!
HOLY--
BRAKAKA BRAKAKA
BRAKAKABRAKAKA
B-DOOOOM
OH MY GOD-- BRUCE? I THOUGHT IT WAS FIREWORKS OUTSIDE...
...BRUCE?

BRAKAKABRAKAKA
BULLOCK, LOOKS LIKE THEY ESCAPED DOWN THE MANHOLE WHILE THIS GUY PROVIDED COVER.
WONDER WHAT THE *REAL BATMAN* WOULD HAVE TO SAY ABOUT THIS.
HOPEFULLY, HE'LL BE ABLE TO DO SOMETHING ABOUT THESE *CHEAP STAND-INS.* BUT WE'RE NOT WAITING.
I WANT EVERY EXIT POINT WITHIN TWO MILES SEALED AND GUARDED...
"...WE'LL FLUSH THEM OUT LIKE *COCKROACHES.*"
MOVE IT! THEY'LL BE CLOSING IN ON US FROM EVERY ANGLE.
NUMBER THREE, TAKE POINT.
?!
YOU HEAR ME, NUMBER THREE? TAKE POI--

YOU OWE ME SOME ANSWERS...
WHAT THE--?!
...AFTER YOU WAKE UP, OF COURSE.
SMASH

CRACK
The acoustics in these tunnels make it difficult to sneak up on someone.
BRAKAKA BRAKAKA
Advantage: me.
WHUFF

But I can't dodge **bullets** forever.
I need to end this before they end me.
BOOM, BATMAN. YOU'RE *DEAD.*
Some kind of rip cord?
VIIPPP
Why did he just--
BOOOMM

--kill himself?!
There's the alpha dog--running away.
FWIPP
He's strong. But not **my level** strong.

URGHHHH!
OOHF!
BAFF
VIP
Another rip cord!
BOOOSHH
WELL DONE, MEN.

VERY WELL DONE, INDEED.
POOF
THERE! I SEE ONE OF 'EM!
HOLD YOUR FIRE! I THINK THAT'S THE *REAL DEAL.*
DOES IT MATTER?
APPARENTLY, IT DOES. WORD FROM ON HIGH AT CITY HALL IS TO LAY OFF... FOR NOW.

GOTHAM CITY POLICE DEPARTMENT.
WE GET THOSE BODIES ID'D YET, SGT. BULLOCK?
NO SUCH LUCK, BOSS. BUT THE MEDICAL EXAMINER SEEMS TO THINK THE FAUX-BATS ARE RELATED TO EACH OTHER.
THINKS THEY COULD BE BROTHERS. BUT, HELL, HE'S PIECING THEM BACK TOGETHER LIKE A JIGSAW PUZZLE--
BLOWING YOURSELF UP WILL HAVE THAT EFFECT.
CLAK
THESE CRIMINALS SACRIFICING THEIR LIVES FOR THAT CARGO IS ONLY THE FIRST PIECE OF A MUCH LARGER PUZZLE, BATMAN.
WHAT THOSE MEN STOLE ORIGINATED FROM THE DUNHILL LABORATORY DOWNSTATE.
THE SAME DUNHILL LAB THAT WAS CLOSED DOWN THIS AFTERNOON DUE TO A RADIATION ACCIDENT.
HERE ARE THE CRIME SCENE FILES.
JUST A WARNING--THE PHOTOS ARE GRUESOME. THE LEAD PHYSICIST'S BODY WAS FOUND... MELTED.
MELTED?
YEAH. LIKE CHEESE PIZZA.
THAT'S EVERYTHING WE KNOW ON THAT FILE. I'M CURIOUS TO HEAR WHAT YOU CAN MAKE OF IT.

THE BATCAVE.
THIS ALL LEADS BACK TO THE DUNHILL LABORATORY, ALFRED. YOU MIGHT HAVE READ ABOUT THEM IN THE NEWS ABOUT A YEAR AGO.
AH, YES. I REMEMBER, MASTER BRUCE.
BUILDING A VARIATION OF THAT DREADED BLACK HOLE CREATOR, WAS IT?
A HADRON COLLIDER. AN ATOM SMASHER.
SO FAR THE PHYSICISTS ATTEMPTING TO PROVE TIME TRAVEL AND THE DISCOVERY OF PARALLEL DIMENSIONS HAVE ONLY BEEN HIT WITH SETBACKS.
TIME TRAVEL? PARALLEL DIMENSIONS, SIR?
STRANGE AS IT SOUNDS, MANY A GREAT MIND HAS TOILED OVER THOSE VERY THEORIES SINCE EINSTEIN PROPOSED THAT TIME TRAVEL WAS POSSIBLE.
ONLY THING IS, THE CLOSER THEY GET TO AN ANSWER, THE MORE COSTLY IT GETS.
ANY IDEAS AS TO WHAT WAS BEING TRANSPORTED FROM DUNHILL THAT CREATED SO MUCH CARNAGE TODAY, SIR?
PROFESSOR DUNHILL SAYS IT WAS A HIGHLY SENSITIVE, CORROSIVE AND RADIOACTIVE SUBSTANCE. HE WAS SHIPPING IT OFF TO S.T.A.R. LABS TO BE FURTHER ANALYZED AFTER BREAKING DOWN ITS ATOMIC STRUCTURE.
THAT'S WHEN THE HIJACK OCCURRED.
BUT SOMEONE KNEW IT WAS EN ROUTE. SOMEONE ON THE INSIDE HAD TO BE WORKING ON THIS.
GREEN LAWN BUILDER-- SIGN UP NOW FOR NEXT SEASON'S DEALS!
CLICK HERE
sign up or create a new account
THESE CRIME SCENE FILES AREN'T GIVING ME MUCH IN THE WAY OF...
H&M
...LEADS.

HM Industries set up a workshop inside Wayne Tower. They've been there for the last nine months.
Hugh Marder, their president, a man I actually like, has been working feverishly to develop technology that'll aid in the development of cancer drugs.
I trusted he was working on the technology he so enthusiastically put all his weight behind.
But this...
...some kind of fluid I'm standing in. A puddle-- mixed with blood.
Some sort of energy...it's drifting as if there's an airflow or wind pushing it.
CLIK

Spectrum analysis reveals that someone's been here. They're still here.
There's a humming, I can feel the vibrations under my feet.
SECURITY ROOM SIX-FIFTY-TWO. PROTOCOL EIGHT-FIFTY-SEVEN.
OPEN.
ZSHFFFFFFF
Some form of the Large Hadron Collider. And fully operational--proton energy is growing within its core.
WHO'S HERE?!
MARDER...?
H-H-ELP... ME...H-HE-L-LP ME-E-E...
...BATMAN-- S-SAVE Y-YOURSELFFF...! BEHIND YOU!

YOU'RE SERIOUSLY ONE UNLUCKY PERSON, BATMAN. NOT MANY LIVE TO CROSS MR. TOXIC'S PATH MORE THAN ONCE.
ZZZATCCHHCHCH
ESPECIALLY WHEN INTERFERING WITH BUSINESS SO IMPORTANT TO ME.
MR. MARDER, HERE, WILL BE A PRIME EXAMPLE OF THAT.
TONIGHT, ONE CRUSADER DIES--WHILE ANOTHER IS BORN!

FLorea

WAYNE TOWER.
HUGH MARDER'S EXPERIMENTAL LAB...
Blinding energy... almost...
...paralyzing every muscle...
...only one chance... to see if Lucius's prototype energy deflector's operational...
FLAK
...Mr. Toxic will kill me if it fails...
...but that's a big if...

Batman in DETECTIVE COMICS
RADIOACTIVE!
Written by TONY S. DANIEL
Pencilled by JULIO FERREIRA and EDUARDO PANSICA
Inks by JULIO FERREIRA and EBER FERREIRA
colors by TOMEU MOREY
lettering by JARED K. FLETCHER
cover by TONY S. DANIEL, SANDU FLOREA and TOMEU MOREY
...thank you, Lucius.

SZAFFF
ARGH!

YOU'RE THE MAN FROM THE SEWERS--MR. TOXIC, IS IT?
SOK
YOU HAVE NO IDEA WHAT YOU'RE INTERFERING WITH, BATMAN!
I'M SURE YOU'LL FILL ME IN.
OUT OF MY WAY!
NNG!
He weighs a ton. Feels like I'm running up against a brick wall.
Could be the radiation affecting me.
He needs to go down fast. I've got to get to Hugh Marder in time.

Moving... in... slow... motion...
WHUDD
...can't move... fast enough...
KRAK
WHACK
YOU'RE TOO SLOW. AND YOU'LL ONLY GET SLOWER.
HERE, WATCH ME PROVE IT TO YOU.
SEE? HOPE YOU'RE NOT OVERLY FOND OF THAT HEAD OF YOURS--
THAP

MY PHYSICAL BODY MAY BE MOMENTARILY IMPAIRED--
--BUT MY MIND'S ALWAYS THINKING AHEAD.
SMASH
>KOFF KOFF KOFF< I-- CAN'T BREATHE! LOOK WHAT YOU'VE DONE TO ME!
MARDER?! BUT HOW--
I'VE ACCOMPLISHED WHAT I NEEDED TO. YOU'RE TOO LATE, BATMAN.
SHOOMPHH

AARGGH!
How are there two Marders?
The Collider looks like it's about to self-destruct--
--need to shut it down!
NOOO!
Can't stop the system. It's overloading!
999,999
BAZHOOOM

WHAT'D YOU DO? WHAT JUST HAPPENED?
IT'S TOO LATE, BATMAN. I HAVE THE POWER. FINALLY... I HAVE IT...
AGHHFF!
WHAT POWER? WHAT--
--NO.
He...Marder's dead.

EVACUATE THE TOWER! THERE'S A HIGH LEVEL OF RADIOACTIVITY PRESENT!
MR. FOX-- GET YOURSELF OUT!
No time to answer questions...feeling too...weak...
KARASH
SHLOMF
CLAK
I'LL REEL YOU IN, SIR! HANG TIGHT.
Thank God for Alfred.

THE BATCAVE...
"JUST A FEW MOMENTS MORE, MASTER BRUCE... FOR GOOD MEASURE."
THE READING INDICATES RADIOACTIVITY LEVELS ARE HOLDING AT ZERO, BUT WE HAVEN'T REALLY TESTED THIS DECONTAMINATION UNIT BEFORE.
THIS MUST BE WHAT SUPERMAN FEELS LIKE WHEN HE'S EXPOSED TO KRYPTONITE.
LIKE MOVING THROUGH QUICKSAND...
RADIATION WILL DO THAT EVEN TO A RHINOCEROS, MASTER BRUCE.
YOU'LL DO YOUR BODY GOOD WITH A NIGHT'S WORTH OF SLEEP...
MY BODY'S SLOW, ALFRED. NOT MY MIND. I HAVE A LOT OF THINKING TO DO.
MARDER'S LAST WORDS...HE SOUNDED ALMOST ***RELIEVED.***
RELIEVED THAT HE WAS ***DYING,*** SIR?
NO. SOMETHING ABOUT ***POWER.*** THAT HE'D FINALLY ATTAINED IT.
I DON'T KNOW IF HE WAS DELUSIONAL IN HIS FINAL MOMENTS...

"...OR IF IT WAS SOMETHING ELSE ENTIRELY."
WAYNE TOWER, THE NEXT DAY.
THE COUNTY MORGUE SAYS MARDER'S BODY SHOWS SIGNS OF CELLULAR DE-CONSTRUCTION, MR. WAYNE.
IT'S GOING TO TAKE US SOME TIME TO FIGURE OUT WHAT THE *ACTUAL* CAUSE OF DEATH WAS.
BUT WHATEVER THIS MACHINE IS THAT HE BUILT IN OUR LABORATORIES, I'M SURE IT HAD SOMETHING TO DO WITH IT.
IT'S VERY SIMILAR TO THE *LARGE HADRON COLLIDER.* NOT EXACT, BUT MY GUESS IS THAT MARDER WAS USING THIS LAB FOR SIMILAR STUDIES.
TO CREATE A *BLACK HOLE?* WHAT ON EARTH FOR?
THERE ARE MANY THEORIES SURROUNDING THE ORIGINAL MACHINE. ANTIMATTER PROPULSION, INTERSTELLAR SPACE TRAVEL... THE LIST GOES ON.
THE QUEST FOR TRAVELING FASTER THAN THE SPEED OF LIGHT. I GET IT. BUT WHY IS IT *HERE?*
WAS MARDER TESTING IT ON HIMSELF? TRYING TO PROPEL *HIMSELF* THROUGH SPACE?
ANY THEORIES ON WHY ANY SANE MAN WOULD DO THAT, LUCIUS? MY GUESS? THE PARTICLE ACCELERATOR GENERATED *GAMMA RAYS* WHICH LIKELY TORE PROFESSOR MARDER APART, ATOM BY ATOM.
BUT IF HE DID IT TO HIMSELF, HE WAS MOST LIKELY HOPING FOR A DIFFERENT OUTCOME.
MR. WAYNE, THERE'S SOMEONE ON LINE TWO WHO SAYS HE MUST SPEAK WITH YOU.
SAY'S IT'S A MATTER OF *LIFE AND DEATH.* SHOULD I TELL HIM YOU'RE IN A MEETING?
NO, WENDY, I'LL TAKE THE CALL.
HELLO? WHO IS THIS?
WE HAVE TO MEET, MR. WAYNE. TODAY. I CAN'T TALK TO YOU MUCH LONGER OR THEY'LL TRACE THE CALL.
WHAT IS THIS ABOUT?
MARDER-- AND THE HELL HE STILL PLANS TO UNLEASH. MY NAME IS ***PROFESSOR ALAN SMART.***
IF YOU WANT TO SAVE THOUSANDS OF LIVES... YOU'LL FIND ME AT THE DUNHILL LAB.
CLICK
HELLO?

Whatever those Batman impostors stole originated from Dunhill Laboratories yesterday.
And it can't be a coincidence that Dunhill recently had its own radioactive "incident."
DUNHILL
The man I spoke with on the phone claims to be Professor Alan Smart-- who mysteriously disappeared without a trace nearly a year ago. Presumed dead.
Since he apparently doesn't exist, I'm meeting with the man running Dunhill, Professor Arthur Manhart.
GOOD AFTERNOON, MR. WAYNE.
COME IN BEFORE THE N.I.H. COMES AND KICKS US ALL OUT AGAIN.
I'M SURPRISED BY YOUR VISIT TODAY, BUT YOU'RE CERTAINLY WELCOME CONSIDERING OUR RECENT TRAGEDIES.
I'M LOOKING FOR SOME ANSWERS SURROUNDING THE ACCIDENT THAT HAPPENED HERE YESTERDAY. I UNDERSTAND THERE WERE SOME FATALITIES.
THE VICTIMS WERE DESCRIBED IN THE MEDIA AS HAVING BEEN MELTED.
ESPIONAGE! IT HAD TO BE, MR. WAYNE. I'M SURE YOU UNDERSTAND THE RABIDLY COMPETITIVE NATURE OF OUR INDUSTRY.
EVEN OUR TOUGHEST SCREENING MEASURES CAN'T STAND UP TO A DETERMINED INFILTRATOR. A SPY!
A SPY? LIKE THE KIND PROFESSOR ALAN SMART WAS ACCUSED OF BEING?
WE HAD QUESTIONS FOR SMART. HE DISAPPEARED BEFORE ANY COULD BE ANSWERED.
WHY DO YOU BRING HIM UP? HE'S BEEN GONE FOR QUITE SOME TIME.
NO REASON. JUST FOUND IT STRANGE THAT HE DISAPPEARED AFTER BEING LINKED TO SPYING FOR LEXCORP.
I ADMIT, WE NEVER FOUND ANY PROOF OF HIS INDISCRETIONS. BUT I'M AFRAID WE'LL NEVER KNOW WHAT HAPPENED TO THE PROFESSOR.
HOW DANGEROUS IS THE MATERIAL RESIDUE YOU WERE SHIPPING TO S.T.A.R. LABS YESTERDAY? HIGHLY RADIOACTIVE?
WE FOUND THE SAME RESIDUE INSIDE OUR OWN HADRON COLLIDER. WE HAVE NO IDEA WHAT IT IS OR WHERE IT CAME FROM.
INTERESTING... WE SUSPECT IT MIGHT HAVE BEEN WHAT KILLED MY PROFESSORS.
THANKS FOR LETTING ME TAKE A SPECIMEN. I'LL REPORT TO YOU ANYTHING MY LAB HYPOTHESIZES, PROFESSOR.

SHORT CONVERSATION, MASTER WAYNE?
SHORT IS ALL I HAVE TIME FOR, ALFRED. I NEED TO GET TO THE PAY PHONE PROFESSOR SMART CALLED FROM THIS MORNING.
WERE YOU ABLE TO DETERMINE THE LOCATION?
OF COURSE. AND IT'S CLOSER THAN YOU THINK.
WAIT HERE, ALFRED.
AS YOU WISH...
SIR! PLEASE HOLD UP!
YOU'VE GOT LEGS. FOLLOW ME, BOY.
PROFESSOR SMART?
NOT SO LOUD! THERE ARE PEOPLE WHO THINK I'M DEAD.
I'VE WORKED PRETTY HARD TO KEEP IT THAT WAY.

YOU WANTED TO TALK TO ME. WELL, I'M HERE, PROFESSOR SMART. WHAT DO YOU HAVE TO TELL ME?
IT'S INSIDE WAYNE INDUSTRIES. INSIDE THE LAB THAT YOU ALLOWED HUGH MARDER TO CONSTRUCT.
WHAT IS, EXACTLY?
THE PARTICLE ACCELERATOR. MARDER'S NEARLY FOUND A WAY TO TURN MATTER INTO ANTIMATTER.
HE'S BEEN WORKING ON A FORM OF MULTIPHASE TRAVEL THAT, IN SOME THEORIES, HAS THE EFFECT OF FORWARD TIME TRAVEL.
THAT'S NOT POSSIBLE. MAN CAN'T TRAVEL THROUGH TIME ALONE... MAYBE INSIDE A VEHICLE. I UNDERSTAND THE THEORY OF ANTIMATTER SPACE PROPULSION, BUT--
HUGH'S TESTED HIS THEORIES ON HIS OWN CLONES. I EVEN HELPED HIM DEVELOP THEIR BIOLOGY. THEY'RE JUST LIKE HIM... BUT THEY DECAY.
FIRST THEIR BODIES, THEN THEIR MINDS.
WAIT, PROFESSOR--NONE OF WHAT YOU'VE TOLD ME SOUNDS SCIENTIFICALLY POSSIBLE... OR EVEN SANE.
AND WHY SEEK ME OUT? WHY NOT GO TO THE AUTHORITIES?
BECAUSE MARDER HAS ALREADY STARTED HIS CELLULAR REGENERATION PROCESS. I BELIEVE YOUR LAB STILL MIGHT HAVE THE NECESSARY TOOLS TO NEUTRALIZE HIS CELL GROWTH.
HUGH MARDER DIED LAST NIGHT.
BUT WAS IT REALLY MARDER? OR ONE OF HIS CARBON COPIES?
I'VE SAVED THIS FOR THE F.B.I., A RECORDING WHICH DETAILS EVERYTHING ABOUT MARDER'S PARTICLE ACCELERATION PROJECT.
BUT I DON'T TRUST THE F.B.I....

GOTHAM CITY MORGUE.
"...I TRUST YOU."
HERE'S NUMBER FIVE. NICE AND CLEAN.
I ASSUME YOU MEAN HE'S BEEN DECON-TAMINATED?
CLEANED UP BY HAZMAT. CAN'T GET ANY CLEANER THAN THAT!
THE FIRST FOUR LOOK-ALIKES YESTERDAY AND NOW THIS ONE TODAY. HOW ODD.
YOU TELL ANYONE ABOUT THIS YET?
JUST THE POLICE COMMISSIONER. HE WANTS TO SEE PICS.
QUINTUPLETS-- UNLESS THERE ARE MORE. AND ALL DEAD WITHIN TWENTY-FOUR HOURS OF EACH OTHER.
WELL, THE FIRST FOUR DIED IN WHAT THE NEWS IS CALLING A SUICIDE MISSION. THIS LAST ONE WAS SOME SORT OF ELITE PHYSICIST. A PROFESSOR HUGH MARDER.
SO HIS BROTHERS GO NUTS AND DRESS UP AS BATMAN WHILE HE PRACTICALLY MELTS INSIDE SOME SORT OF NUCLEAR MICROWAVE? THAT'S ALL SORTS OF NUTS.
WHAT'S MORE NUTS, BRIAN, IS THAT THEIR HEIGHTS AND WEIGHTS ARE EXACT. I WANT TO TAKE SOME SAMPLES FOR DNA TESTS.
I'VE NEVER SEEN ANYTHING LIKE THIS BEFORE. AND I DOUBT ANYONE ELSE HAS EITHER.

FEELS LIKE A DRAFT. IS THERE A WINDOW OP--
AARRGHHH!
YAAAGGHH!
WHAT...WHAT HAPPENED?
WAKE UP, MARDER. YOU'RE SO CLOSE TO YOUR ULTIMATE SUCCESS.

I'M ALIVE... BUT... THIS IS ALL WRONG...
IT WAS A SIMPLE CALCULATION ERROR. WE MUST HURRY TO DUNHILL LABS IF WE ARE TO SAVE YOUR LIFE.
WHUMP
I... I CAN'T BREATHE, YOU IMBECILE! DON'T JUST STAND--THERE! HUHHHHH!
HELP... HACK HACK KOFF ...HELP... ME...!
IF YOU DIE, I DIE. AND I WILL LIVE. ONE WAY OR ANOTHER.
PUT THIS ON. IT WILL KEEP YOU FROM SUCCUMBING TO THE RADIUM.

GOTHAM CITY MORGUE, A SHORT WHILE LATER...
"HUGH MARDER'S BODY IS MISSING.
"SURVEILLANCE VIDEO SHOWS HE WAS WHEELED IN, BUT THERE'S NO SIGN OF HIM EVER LEAVING."
MORGUE
HAZMAT QUARANTINED WHAT WAS LEFT OF THE TWO VICTIMS. NOTHING BUT BONES AND FLESH.
BUT I UNDERSTAND THAT BEFORE HAZMAT COULD ZIP UP THE BODY BAGS, THEY PRACTICALLY DIS-INTEGRATED.
OR MELTED?
HM. LIKE THE VICTIMS OF DUNHILL LAB THE OTHER DAY.
DID YOU KNOW HOW CLOSELY THESE MEN RESEMBLED EACH OTHER?
NOT TILL I ARRIVED HERE. I RECEIVED A CALL FROM THE DOCTOR ON DUTY. HE SAID THEY LOOKED "SIMILAR."
THIS ISN'T SIMILAR. THIS IS EXACTLY THE SAME.
I NEED TO KNOW JUST HOW SIMILAR THEY ARE.

THE BATCAVE...
Professor Smart's accusation that Marder made clones of himself is starting to look more like fact than fiction.
Their DNA is nearly identical. Save for the presence of positrons.
Could they have all been exposed to the radiation from the hadron collider's particle accelerator?
Is it possible that Marder found a way to create multiple copies of himself? But for what purpose?
Whatever he's trying to do...I don't think it's going according to plan.
The positrons in the sample from the morgue seem to attract the radiated protons from the sample Professor Manhart gave me at Dunhill...but it's causing an aggressive reaction.
Better contain it before--
SPLK
The gas is liquefying!

Got to get back. It's out of control!
Got to--
GAARRGGHH!

2012
S.Florea

2012

THE BATCAVE.
CRASH
Can't breathe... must get...
...the radiation poisoning antidote...
...no!
Some kind of chemical reaction...
...GOING... NUMB...CAN'T... MAKE IT...

Batman in
DETECTIVE
comics
THE KILLER INSIDE
Written and Pencilled by TONY S. DANIEL
Inks by RICHARD FRIEND
colors by TOMEU MOREY
lettering by JARED K. FLETCHER
cover by TONY S. DANIEL, SANDU FLOREA and TOMEU MOREY

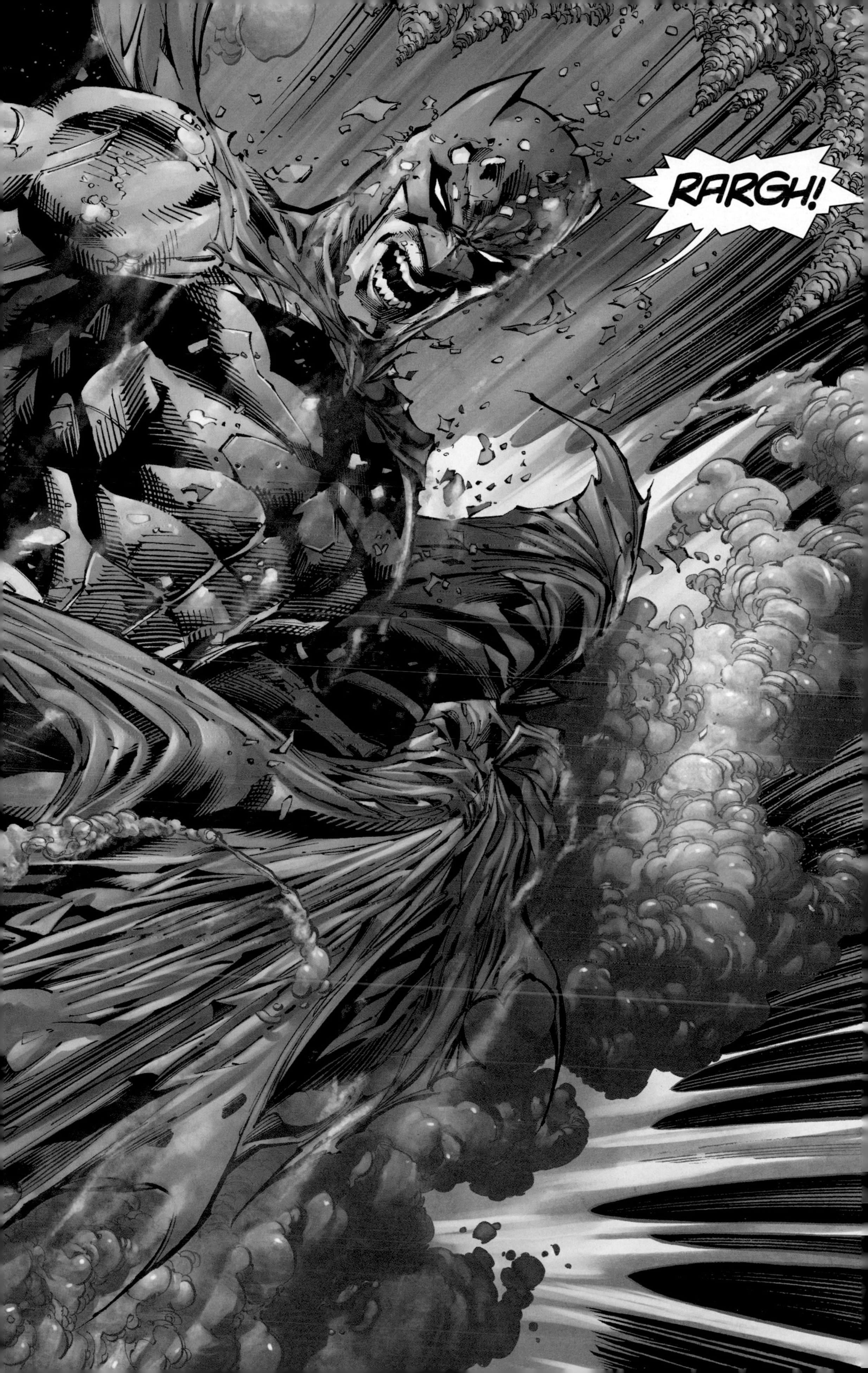
RARGH!

GRGH!
CLANK
SHOOOSHHHH
SIR! ALLOW ME--
NO, ALFRED. STAY BACK!
I DON'T KNOW WHAT WE'RE DEALING WITH...
...YET.

THE ORGANISM I WAS TESTING FROM DUNHILL LABORATORIES HAD A STRONG REACTION TO THE ANTIDOTE.
IT SOAKED UP THE CHEMICALS LIKE A *SPONGE.*
GOOD WORK, SIR. YOU KNEW THE ORGANISM WOULD ALSO *CONSUME* THE FLAMES AND DESTROY ITSELF?
MORE OF A *LAST DITCH* EFFORT, ALFRED. I GOT LUCKY THIS TIME.
IT APPEARS TO BE DISINTEGRAT-ING.
QUICK, GET ME A GRADE-THREE CANISTER.
I DON'T HAVE MUCH TIME.

DUNHILL LABORATORIES.
LOOKS LIKE YOU DID A GOOD JOB CLEANING UP THE DAMAGE HERE, PROFESSOR MANHART...
...I'LL NOTIFY THE CITY YOU HAVE THE "ALL CLEAR" TO REOPEN FOR WORK.
THANK YOU, INSPECTOR, BUT I'M AFRAID THE DAMAGE DONE IS BEYOND CLEANING UP.
THE FAMILIES OF OUR STAFF HAVE A LONG ROAD OF HEALING AHEAD OF THEM...WE HAVE SEVERAL FUNERALS TOMORROW.
HAVE THE POLICE BACKED OFF?
YES. THANK YOU FOR YOUR HELP, JEFFREY. LORD KNOWS I ALREADY HAVE MY HANDS FULL EXPLAINING THINGS TO THE N.I.H. AND THE D.H.S.
IT'S GOOD TO HAVE FRIENDS LIKE YOU...IN HIGH PLACES.
TAP TAP
YOU'RE A GOOD MAN, PROFESSOR MANHART. SAY HELLO TO THE WIFE AND KIDS.
BA-DOOOMM

GET UP, MANHART. I'VE RETURNED.
MR. TOXIC! NO...IT'S NOT READY!
YOUR ATOMIC STRUCTURE WILL CAUSE THE PARTICLE ACCELERATOR TO SELF-DESTRUCT! I WILL NOT BE RESPONSIBLE FOR--
FOR KILLING THOUSANDS? HUNDREDS OF THOUSANDS?
YOU WON'T. I WILL TAKE FULL RESPONSIBILITY FOR ANY COLLATERAL DAMAGE THAT MAY RESULT FROM MY ACTIONS.
I NEED TO BE REPAIRED AT ANY COST!
DO AS YOU'RE TOLD, MANHART--OR I'LL MAKE SURE ALL OF GOTHAM CITY IS SUCKED INTO A BLACK HOLE!

INSIDE THE BATCAVE...
I FINALLY HAVE THE HOMELESS MAN'S PEN DEVICE WORKING, MASTER BRUCE.
THOUGH IT WASN'T AN EASY TASK--IT WAS CAKED WITH A YEAR'S WORTH OF...ICK.
A CLOGGED PEN, SO TO SPEAK. PERHAPS SOME TYPE OF SECURITY MEASURE.
GOOD WORK, ALFRED. PROFESSOR SMART WAS HOMELESS BY CHOICE. HE FELT THE SECRETS HE UNCOVERED WHILE WORKING FOR DUNHILL PUT HIS LIFE IN JEOPARDY.
OH MY. A HOLOGRAM?
IT'S PROFESSOR SMART...
HE LOOKS SO DIFFERENT AFTER A GOOD SHAVE--I HARDLY RECOGNIZED HIM.
SHH...
TO WHOM IT MAY CONCERN...
...I HOPE THIS MESSAGE REACHES THE PROPER CHANNELS WHO CAN STOP THE MADNESS WITHIN THE RESEARCH FACILITY OF DUNHILL LABOR-ATORIES.
SOMEONE NEEDS TO BE ALERTED TO THE DEVIOUS HORRORS BEING PERFORMED IN THE NAME OF SCIENCE BY PROFESSOR HUGH MARDER.
HIS ATTEMPTS TO CURE HIS OWN GENETIC DISEASE HAVE DRIVEN HIM TO INSANITY. HE USED THE PARTICLE ACCELERATOR ON CADAVER D.N.A. AND SPLICED IT WITH HIS OWN.
THE RESULTS ARE SHORT-LIVED REPLICAS WHICH HE USES TO FURTHER HIS...STUDIES.

I TRIED TO STOP MARDER, BUT HE THREATENED TO CUT OFF FUNDING TO DUNHILL.
HE MADE IT **VERY** CLEAR HIS FINANCIERS WERE **NOT** TO BE TRIFLED WITH.
HE THREATENED THAT I HAD **NO** CHOICE BUT TO OVERSEE A NEW GENE-ALTERING EXPERIMENT HE PLANNED FOR HIMSELF.
I WARNED HIM THE PARTICLE ACCELERATOR WAS NOT BUILT FOR HIS INTENTIONS AND THAT HE WOULD LIKELY **DIE.**
BUT THIS DIDN'T DETER A MAN WHO WAS ALREADY DYING.
HE EMERGED FROM THE PARTICLE ACCELERATOR A VERY... **DIFFERENT** BEING. SINCE THAT DAY, I RAN AND **NEVER** LOOKED BACK.
I CONSIDER MYSELF PARTIALLY RESPONSIBLE FOR CREATING THIS MONSTER. I HAD MY CHANCE TO RID THE EARTH OF HIM WHILE HE WAS INSIDE THE LARGE HADRON COLLIDER. **THAT** IS MY **BIGGEST** REGRET.
HIS BODY **ABSORBED** THE RADIATION AND, IN FACT, IS LIVING OFF IT. I FEAR IT'S ONLY A MATTER OF TIME BEFORE HE BECOMES A WALKING **ATOMIC BOMB.**

DUNHILL LABORATORIES.
YOU'RE ASKING ME TO HELP YOU COMMIT MASS MURDER!
NOT IF THE GENETIC COCKTAIL YOU DEVELOPED BEHIND MY BACK REACTS PROPERLY WHEN I ABSORB IT.
BUT...YOU LEFT DUNHILL TO COMPLETE YOUR WORK AT WAYNE ENTERPRISES! I-I--
LET'S NOT FORGET WHICH ONE OF US IS THE ORIGINAL, MR. TOXIC.
I AM NO LONGER A CARBON COPY OF YOU! I AM YOUR EQUAL NOW, MARDER!
I SAVED YOUR LIFE!
YOUR WORK IS UNFINISHED!

GOTHAM CITY.
I'VE DETECTED AN EXTREMELY HIGH POWER SURGE WITHIN THE STRUCTURE OF THE DUNHILL LABORATORIES, BATMAN.
AND I KNOW WHY, ALFRED. CAN YOU TAP INTO THE DUNHILL VIDEO FEEDS?
I'M AFRAID MY ATTEMPTS HAVE NOT BEEN SUCCESSFUL. THEIR SURVEILLANCE HAS GONE BLACK!
SEND AN ANONYMOUS WARNING TO HAZMAT AND THE COMMISSIONER, JUST IN CASE.
SHOULD I ALERT OUR ALLIES IN THE AREA FOR ASSISTANCE? YOU'RE STILL A BIT GROGGY FROM EARLIER THIS EVENING.
"NO, ALFRED..."

...I'VE GOT THIS.
VRMMMMMMMMMM
FWWWWOOOOHHSSSH
SSSSHHHHH

WE ARE READY, MANHART. START THE COLLIDER.
NOW, YOU FOOL!
Y-YES. IT'S NOT LIKE TURNING ON A DAMNED LIGHT!
LET THE GOOD MAN WORK. UNLIKE YOU, I CANNOT AFFORD ANOTHER MISTAKE.
NO ONE SHOULD HAVE THIS KIND OF POWER. IT'S N-NOT NATURAL! IT CAN'T HAPPEN...
DO NOT FAIL ME OR I WILL MAKE CERTAIN THAT ALL OF GOTHAM CITY SINKS INTO THE ABYSS!
BETTER GOTHAM THAN THE WHOLE COUNTRY!

PROFESSOR-- NO!
CRAAA
IT'S TOO LATE, BATMAN!

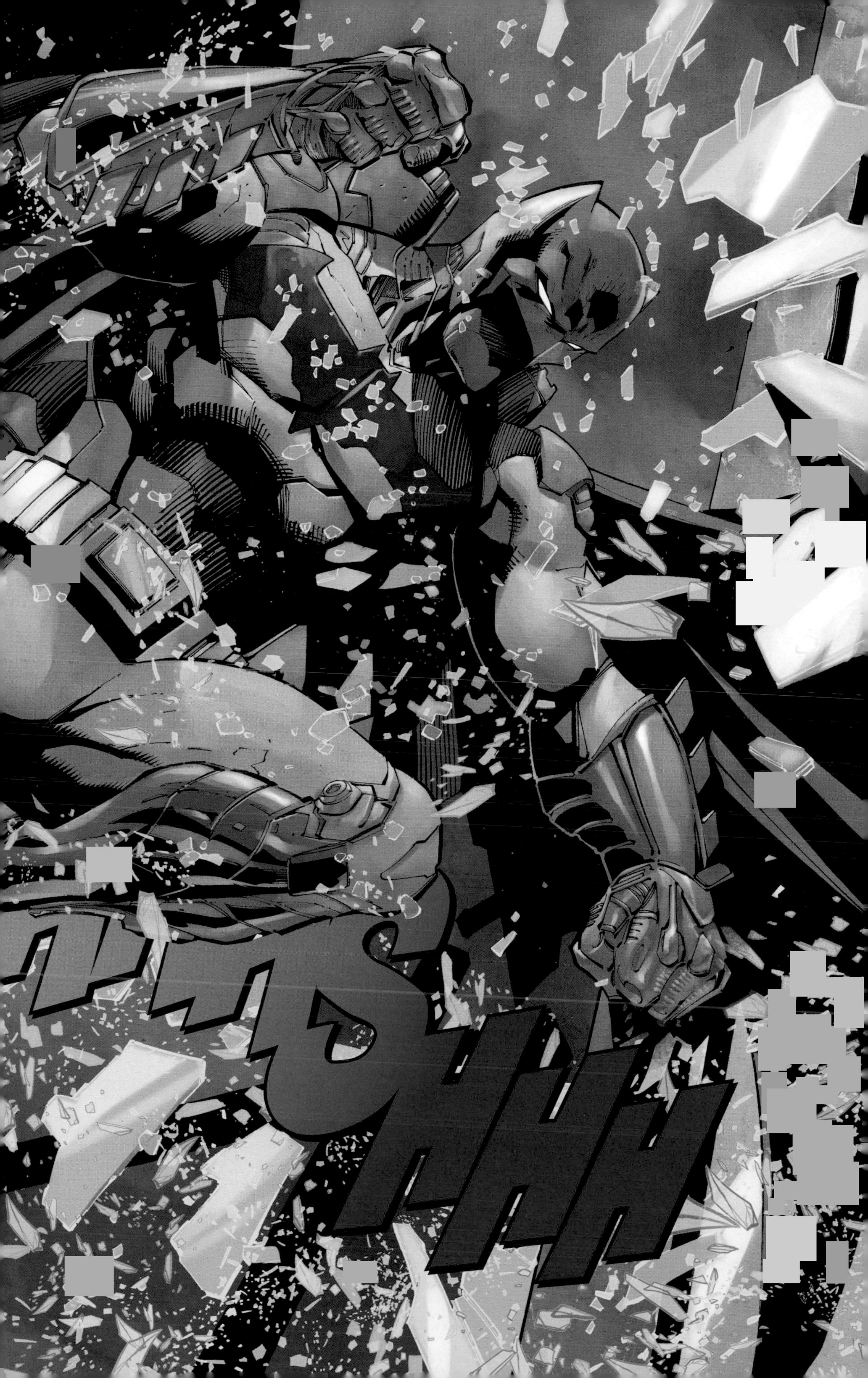
SHHH

NO! GET AWAY!
ARGGH!
The same chemical reaction I witnessed in the Batcave!
FOOOM

Some kind of-- abomination!
BRASH
MARDER?
HELP ME,
BEFORE IT'S TOO LATE!
I have only one shot at this...
...with the chemical reaction creating a physical mutation...
FWOOOSH

THOOM
THOOM
THOOM
THOOM
RAGGH!
THE ORGANISM SUCKS UP SUBATOMIC ENERGY. BUT I DISCOVERED WHEN IT'S COMBINED WITH INTENSE HEAT, IT DRIES OUT--
--NEUTRALIZING ITS ABSORPTION ABILITIES AND REJECTING ITS OWN ENERGY.

WHAT DID YOU DO TO IT?!
I DRIED OUT A SPONGE.
MARDER'S EXPERIMENT MAY VERY WELL KILL HIM. BUT FOR NOW, HE'S RENDERED HARMLESS.
B-BATMAN...? WHAT--WHAT DID YOU--?
SOMETHING I HOPE I DON'T LIVE TO REGRET.

I SAVED YOUR LIFE.

2012
S.Flora

ARKHAM ASYLUM. GOTHAM CITY.
I'M VERY PROUD OF YOUR PROGRESS, MR. SIONIS. IT'S BEEN NEARLY A MONTH SINCE YOU ASKED ME TO TRY ON THAT DREADED BLACK MASK.
I'D VENTURE TO SAY YOU'VE MADE A BREAKTHROUGH. ENOUGH SO THAT I MAY RECONSIDER MOVING YOU BACK INTO THE GENERAL POPULATION.
VRROOOOOOM

It was a great risk you took by letting me reunite with my old partner... with my *mask.*
Not only did the mask and I help rid the Asylum from those nasty *owl creatures...*
...but the incident allowed me to come to terms with my own *dependency issues.*
BUT THAT'S IN THE *PAST,* ROMAN. TODAY, AND EVERY DAY MOVING FORWARD, IS ABOUT THE *FUTURE* AND YOUR GOOD HEALTH.
YOU'LL BE A PRIME EXAMPLE OF HOW MY TREATMENT METHODS REALLY *DO* CORRECT BEHAVIORAL DISABILITIES.
You know, more so than others, how *powerful* the lure of that wretched black mask can be. I thank you for pulling me out of the abyss, Dr. Arkham.
You saved my life.
IT'S NOTHING THAT I'M NOT TRAINED TO DO, ROMAN.
Imagine the destruction that horrid thing could do in the *wrong hands.*
You...you put it away, didn't you?
PUT IT AWAY? WHY-- YES. I THINK I-- NO. NO, *NO*--I'M SURE IT'S SECURE.
Fool! Where is it?
DR. ARKHAM? SIR?
CALM DOWN, ROMAN. IT'S JUST WHERE YOU...
...JUST WHERE YOU TOLD ME...
DR. ARKHAM. SNAP OUT OF IT.

YOU LITTLE LIAR! WHAT DID YOU DO TO ME?! WHAT DID YOU MAKE ME--?
ROMAN SIONIS GOT IN YOUR HEAD, DR. ARKHAM. YOU'VE BEEN HAD.
COMMISSIONER GORDON...
HOW LONG HAS SIONIS BEEN GONE?
SINCE THE NIGHT OF THE OWLS.
IN THE CHAOS, HE SOMEHOW GOT HIS HANDS ON THE BLACK MASK. BEING VICTIMIZED BY THE MASK PREVIOUSLY MADE YOU MORE VULNERABLE TO ITS EFFECTS.
HE MADE YOU BELIEVE THAT HE'D REMAINED IN THIS ROOM THESE LAST FEW WEEKS.
YES. I...I REMEMBER. OF COURSE. ORDERLIES, SEE THE COMMISSIONER OUT WHILE I LIE DOWN.
NOT UNTIL I GET SOME ANSWERS FROM YOU, JEREMIAH.
I'LL HELP YOU IF IT MEANS BRINGING ROMAN BACK TO ME.
WHO DID ROMAN CONFIDE IN AT THE ASYLUM?
I NEED TO KNOW WHO HIS FRIENDS ARE.

BLACK OTTER CARNIVAL.

DETECTIVE COMICS PRESENTS BATMAN IN THE ABUSE
TONY S. DANIEL--writer
ROMANO MOLENAAR--penciller pgs 1-17
PERE PEREZ--art pgs 18-38
SANDU FLOREA--inker pgs 1-17
DAVE SHARPE--lettering
ANDREW DALHOUSE--colors
TONY S. DANIEL, SANDU FLOREA and TOMEU MOREY--cover
Mad Bull.
A new ugly in town.
TUNNEL OF LOVE
SHO
I WILL CRUSH YOU LIKE AN INSECT, BATMAN!
RARGHHH!

YOU'VE ALREADY MADE ME LATE!
SLOW DOWN, BIG GUY. YOU'RE GOING TO HURT SOMEONE.
YOURSELF INCLUDED.
Those roller coaster cars--
--no time to slow them down before they get to the broken beams.
Move!
SKREEEEEEEEEEEE
CLANK
CLANK

SQKKKEEEEEEEEEEECH
Mad Bull. He's--
GAHH!
CRACK!
Okay. That didn't go according to plan.

ARKHAM...
ME HELP YOU? HA! I'M SUPPOSED TA ROT IN HERE FOR LIFE IN CASE YOU HADN'T HEARD!
DR. ARKHAM BELIEVES HE CAN REHABILITATE YOU, CLAYFACE. ARE YOU SAYING YOU DON'T THINK THAT'S POSSIBLE?
JERRY ISN'T REHABILITATING SQUAT IN HERE. WE'RE ALL HIS TEST SUBJECTS. PETS!
SO WHILE YOU ROT IN HERE YOU'RE GOING TO JUST LET ROMAN SIONIS PLAY YOU LIKE A FIDDLE WHILE HE GOES FREE?
I THOUGHT YOU WERE BEYOND BEING ANYONE'S USEFUL IDIOT.
HE USED THAT DAMN MASK ON ME. ON ALL OF US! NO ONE REMEMBERS WHAT HAPPENED THAT NIGHT WITH THE OWL ASSASSINS-- THE TALONS.
BUT HE'LL GET WHAT'S COMING TO HIM, EVENTUALLY. HE'S MADE LOADS OF ENEMIES OVER THE YEARS.
BY PLAYING THEM FOR HIS PUPPETS. LIKE HE DID TO YOU.
SHUT YOUR NICOTINE-STAINED PIE-HOLE! NO ONE PLAYS CLAYFACE FOR ANYTHING!
WE ALL HAVE WAYS TO TAKE THE EDGE OFF. I'M SURE YOU'VE GOT YOURS.
I'VE LEARNED TO LIVE WITH THE PAIN. HOW 'BOUT YOU, GORDON?

GOT IT, HARVEY?
'COURSE. RIGHT HERE, COMMISH. JUST A LIL BIT, THOUGH.
WHAT'S THAT YOU GOT?
WHAT'S IT LOOK LIKE TO YOU?
BASIL KARLO
PAIN MEDICATION
GIVE IT TO ME! I'LL KILL EVERYONE YOU'VE EVER KNOWN OR LOVED IF YOU DON'T! I SWEAR IT!
GOOD IDEA YOU HAD THERE, SGT. BULLOCK.
YOU'RE WELCOME!
LET'S TALK ABOUT ROMAN SIONIS SOME MORE. PARTICULARLY PEOPLE HE HAS BUSINESS WITH ON THE OUTSIDE.

THE CARNIVAL...
NO...IT CAN'T BE...
MISS
SNAKEBOY
...THE HEADS ARE GONE!
CRAKK!

LET'S LOSE THE MASK.
CRRUNNCH!
GUH! THE MASK! THE--
CRUNNCH!
His eyes are cloudy, unfocused.
Under some kind of hypnotism.
I know that gaze.
The samples I'll take will point to one man.
I'm sure of it...

WAYNE MANOR.
...the Black Mask.
GOOD MORNING, ALFRED. YOU HAVE SOMETHING FOR ME?
SIR! AS USUAL, YOUR ASSUMPTION IS CORRECT.

SO THE HYPNOTIC MATERIALS INSIDE MAD BULL'S MASK *MATCH* THE TRACE RESIDUE FROM THE SAWED-OFF CAROUSEL ANIMAL HEADS.
IT'S SIMILAR ENOUGH. THOUGH NOT QUITE EXACT.
THE HIGH TRACES OF HYOSCINE ARE THE COMMON DENOMINATOR, HOWEVER.
THANKS FOR THE LEG WORK, ALFRED. MAYBE I SHOULD HAVE A SUIT MADE UP FOR *YOU.*
I DON'T FANCY CAPES MUCH, MASTER BRUCE. AND THOUGH I ENJOYED THE THEATRE WHEN I WAS YOUNG, I ALWAYS AVOIDED DRESSING UP FOR COSTUME PARTIES.
I REMEMBER FINDING IT A RATHER GARISH CUSTOM.
WE ALL AVOIDED SOMETHING IN OUR YOUTH, ALFRED. I AVOIDED DARK PLACES AT ONE TIME. BUT THESE DAYS...
...I AVOID PEOPLE TRYING TO GET INTO MY MIND.

SO, WHO WAS IN THE MAD BULL'S MIND, SIR? DO YOU PRESUME THE BLACK MASK?
THE ANSWER DEPENDS ON WHO'S RESPONSIBLE FOR HIDING THE ORIGINAL MASKS OF THE FALSE FACE SOCIETY AT BLACK OTTER'S TRAVELING CARNIVAL THESE LAST FEW YEARS.
I WAS UNDER THE IMPRESSION THAT THE FALSE FACE SOCIETY DISAPPEARED WHEN ROMAN SIONIS WAS PUT OUT OF COMMISSION.
SOMEONE HELPED DISMANTLE THE SOCIETY. SOMEONE SIONIS TRUSTED TO HELP HIM IF THE HEAD OF THE SNAKE WAS EVER CUT OFF.
I HAVE A SHORT LIST OF SUSPECTS WHO HAVE A KEEN INTEREST IN HYPNOTICS AND MIND CONTROL.
THEY'VE ALL PROVED TO BE VERY RESOURCEFUL...
...BUT THERE'S ONE WHO TAKES THE CAKE.

THE CARNIVAL...
HEY! WHERE'S MY ASSISTANT?
BUDDY TOOK OFF WHEN THE COPS CAME.
WELL, WHO THE HELL ARE YOU? I NEED TO GET OUT OF HERE. THE COPS ARE BUZZING ALL OVER THIS PLACE!
DON'T WORRY ABOUT BUDDY. HE'S PROBABLY HAVING HIMSELF A GOOD NAP. HE PAID ME TO LOOK AFTER YOU, MR. DEMPSEY. I'LL GET YOU OUT OF HERE EASY-PEASY.
THE COPS ARE EVACUATING THE PARK. HURRY! YOU CAN HIDE IN HERE 'TIL I SWING AROUND WITH MY GOLF CART.
A GOLF CART?
WOULD YOU RATHER WALK OUT?
FINE. JUST AS LONG AS YOU GET ME OUT OF HERE BEFORE--
BEFORE WHAT, MR. DEMPSEY?
F-WHAP
ARGH!

EDGAR DEMPSY, SIGNED, SEALED AND DELIVERED!
GOOD WORK, *DWARF.*
AND TO YOU.
WHAT'S THE MEANING OF--?! *GASP!*

THE B-BLACK MASK...?!
GOOD. HOW KIND OF YOU TO REMEMBER ME AFTER THESE LAST FEW YEARS. I ASSURE YOU, WE WILL GET REACQUAINTED QUICKLY. *VERY* QUICKLY.

GOTHAM CITY POLICE DEPARTMENT.
LATER.
YOU LIKE SNEAKING UP ON PEOPLE, I GET THAT.
BUT ME, TOO?
YOU'RE NOT USED TO IT BY NOW?
HERE'S EVERYTHING I GOT FROM CLAYFACE. TURNS OUT AN OLD ACQUAINTANCE OF ROMAN SIONIS WAS LEFT IN CHARGE OF HIDING THE FALSE FACE SOCIETY MASKS.
HIS NAME'S EDGAR DEMPSEY. THE STORY GOES THAT DEMPSEY WAS PLANNING TO USE THE MASKS TO INFLUENCE MEMBERS OF THE JURY IN ROMAN SIONIS' TRIAL.

"EDGAR LEFT SIONIS HIGH AND DRY, HOWEVER. SIONIS' ONLY CHOICE WAS TO COP AN INSANITY PLEA.
"BUT HIS STAY AT ARKHAM WAS ANYTHING BUT A MENTAL HEALTH SPA. BEING IN SUCH CLOSE PROXIMITY TO THE MASK DROVE HIM INTO A VERY REAL STATE OF INSANITY.
"JUST DESERTS, I SAY.
"SIONIS CLAIMED THE ANIMAL MASKS THE SOCIETY WORE WERE MADE OF THE SAME MATERIAL AS THE BLACK MASK ITSELF.
"THE BOND WAS SO STRONG, IT WAS BELIEVED HE USED THE SOCIETY AS IF THEY WERE HIS OWN APPENDAGES. BUT WITHOUT THE BLACK MASK IN CHARGE, THE SOCIETY FADED AWAY."
AND NOW HE'S LOOKING TO GET THE GANG BACK TOGETHER.
WE'VE GOT AN A.P.B. OUT ON DEMPSEY. THE SOONER WE FIND HIM--ALIVE, HOPEFULLY--THE BETTER OUR CHANCES OF FINDING SIONIS AND HIS BLACK MASK.
ONE THING THAT INTRIGUES ME...WHY DID DEMPSEY DOUBLE-CROSS SIONIS? WHAT DID HE STAND TO GAIN BY CROSSING HIM?
BLACK MASK'S COMPETITION...

"...THE MAD HATTER."
YARGGHGHGHGHGH!
WHY WON'T YOU TALK, YOU LITTLE SNAKE?! CAN'T YOU SEE YOUR MIND IS TOO WEAK TO DEFEND AGAINST MY PROBE?!
PLEASE... STOP...!
MAYBE ALL THE TIME YOU SPENT SEPARATED FROM THE BLACK MASK HAS MADE YOU RUSTY, MR. SIONIS?
DOES THIS LOOK LIKE RUST TO YOU, DWARF?! STRONG MAN-- PUNISH THE NON-BELIEVER NOW!
I OBEY!
CRAASSHHH

YOU MUST HAVE BUILT UP RESISTANCE TO THE SACRED EBONY. HAVE YOU BEEN PLAYING WITH MY MASKS, EDGAR?
N-NO! I SWEAR! I WOULD NEVER STAB YOU IN THE BACK!
THEN WHERE HAVE YOU TAKEN THE MASKS OF THE FALSE FACE SOCIETY?
GA-ACKK!
I'LL T-TAKE YOU THERE. -KK- BUT NOT IF I'M -KEK- DEAD!
I WILL HAVE TO RELY ON YOUR TELLING THE TRUTH BECAUSE I CANNOT SEE INTO YOUR MIND. YOU WILL HAVE TO RELY ON MY MERCY.
GET HIM ON HIS FEET. HE'LL LIVE... FOR NOW.

MEANWHILE, DOWNTOWN...
HUNGH HUNGH HUNGH
GOTCHA!
GOING SOMEWHERE, TWEEDLE-DEE?
AHHGH!
VMMMMMMMMMMMMM

VMMMBBBB
CRASSHH!
I HAVE RIGHTS! I HAVE BIG FRIE--
FRIENDS HAVE A WAY OF NOT BEING AROUND WHEN YOU NEED THEM.
CRASSSH

YOU TWO CAN'T DO ANYTHING IN GOTHAM WITHOUT MY KNOWING ABOUT IT. YOU CAN'T MOVE. YOU CAN'T BREATHE...
...YOU CAN'T *THINK* WITHOUT ME KNOWING ABOUT IT.
WHUMPH
MMPH!
FLK
FLK
THUMP THUMP THUMP THUMP
NOW, LET'S TALK ABOUT WHAT *YOUR* BOSS HAS BEEN UP TO.

GOTHAM MUSEUM OF NATURAL HISTORY.
WHERE ARE MY MASKS, DEMPSEY?
I'LL TAKE YOU TO THEM... K-KEEPING MY PART OF THE BARGAIN, MR. SIONIS.
AND I'LL KEEP MINE. AS LONG AS THERE ARE NO GAMES.
THISSS PLACE GIVES ME THE CREEPSSS...
THAT'S JUST WOLF BOY'S HAIR BRUSHING AGAINST YOUR THIGH AGAIN, SERPENTINE.
GRGHH!
RIGHT UP HERE...JUST AS I KNEW IT WOULD BE.

I SEE LOTS OF MASKS. BUT NONE OF THEM ARE MINE!
WHERE ARE THEY?!
THEY'RE RIGHT IN FRONT OF YOU! HE CHANGED THEM! EXPERIMENTED WITH THEM--
WHO?!
YOU'RE THE FOOL, ROMAN. YOU ALWAYS WERE!
I'LL MAKE YOU EAT YOUR TONGUE, TRAITOR!
DON'T JUST STAND THERE! DIE! DIE! DIE!
YOU CAN'T MAKE ME. I'M UNDER HIS PROTECTION, NOW.

YOU WENT INSANE, ROMAN. WHAT DID YOU EXPECT ME TO DO? I'M NO MATCH FOR YOUR ILK! I NEEDED PROTECTION!
NO!
GRK!
WELL, NOW YOU CAN PUT IT TO USE!
WAIT! NO! ARGKK!
TAKE BACK MY MASKS! CUT THEIR HEADS OFF IF YOU HAVE TO! THE FALSE FACE SOCIETY WILL--
BE NO MORE!

IN THIS STYLE 10/6
THE DWARF WAS YOU--?! MAD HATTER?!
I PREFER "LITTLE PERSON," YOU GHOULISH BAG OF BONES.
AND IT'S NO USE--THE PROPERTIES OF YOUR EBONY MASK WON'T WORK HERE. I'VE ALTERED THE SOCIETY MASKS' CHEMISTRY.
EVEN IF YOU WERE TO TAKE THEM, THEY'D BE OF LITTLE USE TO YOU.
IN FACT, IT'S QUITE THE CONTRARY. YOUR MASK CAN BE OF GREAT USE TO ME.

GRKK!
HNGH!
YOUR FATHER'S COFFIN, WHERE YOU CARVED YOUR EBONY MASK, HAS LONG BEEN ONE OF MY GRAILS. THUS, MAKING *YOU* MY NATURAL ENEMY.
THERE CAN ONLY BE *ONE* MIND CONTROLLER IN GOTHAM CITY.
FINALLY, I HAVE THE *HEAD* OF THE *SNAKE.*
WITH THE FALSE FACE SOCIETY MASKS IN MY POSSESSION, *NO ONE* WILL BE ABLE TO STOP ME!

SHKRASHH!
DON'T BE SO SURE OF YOURSELF, HATTER.
BATMAN!

YOU WON'T TAKE ME BACK TO ARKHAM! I'LL NEVER GO!
CRACK!
BWOOOOSH
They're coming at me from all sides. Have to--

YOU KIDS FIGHT IT OUT. I HAVE WHAT I NEED!
I HAVE THE BATMAN!
CRASSH!
YOU JUST LOST YOUR HAT.
BAM!
NO! I WON'T LET YOU TAKE MY HAT!
IT'S JUST YOU AND ME.
WHICH ONE OF US LIVES? WHICH ONE DIES?
IN THIS STYLE 10/6

YOUR POWERS DON'T WORK HERE! HOW ARE YOU--
WHAT ARE YOU DOING?!

ONE THING YOU SHOULD HAVE LEARNED IS NEVER TO LET YOUR FOOT OFF YOUR OPPONENT'S NECK WHEN HE'S DOWN.
INSTEAD, YOU MAKE HIM CHOKE ON HIS OWN BLOOD!
TAKING BACK WHAT'S MINE--AND THEN SOME!

LESSON TWO IS TO NEVER COME TO GOTHAM WHILE *I'M* HERE.
CRACK!
BAFF
MY MASK! WHAT DID YOU DO?! IT'S CRACKED. IT'S...
...

"I DON'T REMEMBER ANYTHING AFTER THE WHITE LIGHT."
THERE'S NO TRACE OF ANYONE AT THE MUSEUM. BUT THERE'RE DEFINITELY SIGNS OF THE HAVOC THEY CAUSED.
MANY PRICELESS ARTIFACTS, NOT TO MENTION MILLIONS OF DOLLARS IN DAMAGES. BUT THE IMPORTANT THING IS YOU MADE IT OUT OF THERE ALIVE.
YOUR SHEER WILL MUST'VE ENABLED YOU TO SLEEPWALK YOURSELF TO SAFETY.
THERE ARE TOO MANY THINGS WE DON'T KNOW ABOUT THE MASK. IT NEEDS TO BE DESTROYED.
WE CAN'T DESTROY EVIDENCE. BUT I WILL MAKE SURE ROMAN SIONIS NEVER GETS HIS HANDS ON THE MASK AGAIN.
WHERE IS HE NOW?
HERE YOU ARE, BACK HOME IN ARKHAM WHERE YOU BELONG, EH, MR. SIONIS?
HOME SWEET HOME, JUST LIKE I REMEMBER IT, DOCTOR.
WE'VE DONE SOME REMODELING WHILE YOU'VE BEEN OUT. YOU'LL FIND YOUR NEW ROOM A BIT LESS COMFY-- A SMALL SACRIFICE...I'M SURE YOU'LL UNDERSTAND--MADE FOR THE SAKE OF YOUR OWN SECURITY.
IT'LL BE A COLD DAY IN HELL BEFORE HE EVER WALKS OUT OF THERE AGAIN. LOCK HIM UP.
CHA-CHAK!
SIONIS
THE END.

RICHARD FRIEND
2012

RICHARD FRIEND
2012

SOMEWHERE IN THE HIMALAYAS...
TEN YEARS AGO...
NOCK NOCK
I AM SEARCHING FOR THE LEGENDARY SHIHAN MATSUDA.
ZEN-BUDDHIST MONK WARRIOR, MASTER OF MIND CONTROL, TRAINED AT THE HAND OF TIBETAN MAGICIANS AND MARTIAL-ARTS SENSEIS.
SHIHAN MATSUDA IS A MYTH. NO ONE SUCH AS HE LIVES HERE.
SLAM

EEEEK
DC COMICS PROUDLY PRESENTS
BEFORE THE NEW 52
BATMAN IN THE FINAL LESSON

SIX MONTHS LATER...
SFFT
EMBARRASSING.
AGAIN.
SFFT
DIS-GRACEFUL.
AGAIN.
SFFT
SUFFICIENT.
AT LAST YOU ARE PROUD OF ME, SHIHAN.
IT IS TUESDAY. HAVE THE BLADES SHARPENED AGAIN.

KRSH
MIO! WE CANNOT AFFORD FOR YOU TO BREAK ANYTHING ELSE! YOU ARE A BIGGER KLUTZ THAN YOUR MOTHER WAS.
IT'S A GOOD THING SHE'S NOT ALIVE TO SEE HOW POORLY YOU WORK!
NOW HELP THE CUSTOMER.
THE USUAL PRICE?
THAT WILL BE FINE.
WOULD YOU LIKE SOME FRUIT?
NO. NO, THANK YOU.
YOU COME EVERY WEEK. AND YOU NEVER SMILE. SO MUCH DISCIPLINE. SO MUCH DARKNESS.
SOME THINGS ARE WORTH SMILING FOR, NO?
BACK TO WORK, MIO!
ALWAYS YAPPING LIKE A LITTLE DOG.

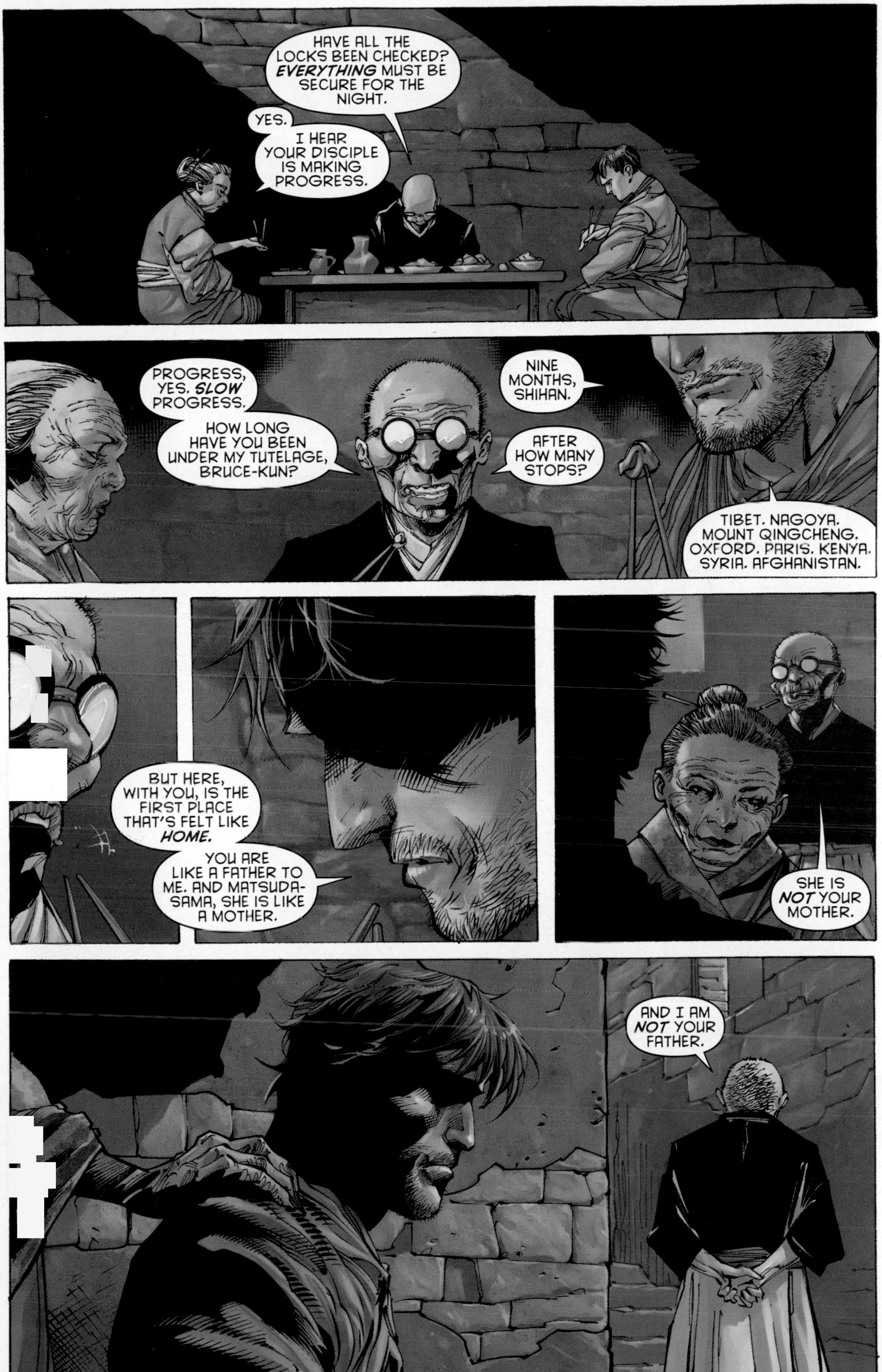
HAVE ALL THE LOCKS BEEN CHECKED? EVERYTHING MUST BE SECURE FOR THE NIGHT.
YES.
I HEAR YOUR DISCIPLE IS MAKING PROGRESS.
PROGRESS, YES. SLOW PROGRESS.
HOW LONG HAVE YOU BEEN UNDER MY TUTELAGE, BRUCE-KUN?
NINE MONTHS, SHIHAN.
AFTER HOW MANY STOPS?
TIBET. NAGOYA. MOUNT QINGCHENG. OXFORD. PARIS. KENYA. SYRIA. AFGHANISTAN.
BUT HERE, WITH YOU, IS THE FIRST PLACE THAT'S FELT LIKE HOME.
YOU ARE LIKE A FATHER TO ME. AND MATSUDA-SAMA, SHE IS LIKE A MOTHER.
SHE IS NOT YOUR MOTHER.
AND I AM NOT YOUR FATHER.

THIS *TONGLEN* HEART-PRACTICE CAN BE VERY DANGEROUS.
YOU MUST SEE ALL THE SUFFERING OF THE WORLD AS BLACK SMOKE. AND YOU MUST TAKE IT IN AND ABSORB IT.
ALL THE WORLD'S HATRED, FEAR, RAGE...
...BREATHE IT IN. IT IS *YOURS* NOW.
AND BREATHE OUT WHITE LIGHT.
RID YOURSELF OF YOUR OWN LOVE, COMPASSION AND JOY. GIVE IT TO THE WORLD.
IT IS ***HONOR.*** IT IS ***SACRIFICE.***
YOU MUST TAKE IN THE DARKNESS FOR OTHERS WHO ARE INCAPABLE OF PROTECTING THEMSELVES FROM IT.
BUT.
IF YOU ARE NOT READY, THIS WILL ***CORRUPT*** YOUR SOUL AND BODY.
WHY MUST I SEND AWAY FROM MYSELF ALL THAT IS LIGHT?
LIGHT IS NOT FOR YOU TO HAVE, BRUCE-KUN. IT IS FOR YOU TO GUARD IN OTHERS.
SHOULDN'T I HOLD SOME WITHIN MYSELF TO ***SHARE*** WITH OTHERS?
NO.
YOU MUST BE ***BETTER*** THAN OTHERS.
INTIMACY IS A ***WEAKNESS.*** IT IS TO BE MORTAL, AND TO BE MORTAL IS TO DIE.
LOVE WILL ERODE YOUR DISCIPLINE. IT WILL ***BLIND*** YOU.
GUARD YOURSELF. LET NO ONE IN. DISTRUST ***EVERYTHING*** AND ***EVERYONE.***
ONLY THEN WILL YOU BECOME A ***TRUE WARRIOR.***

HOW GOES YOUR MEDITATION?
KLK
WELL, MATSUDA-SAMA.
SHIHAN IS TEACHING ME HOW TO GAIN DISTANCE FROM MY EMOTIONS.
DISTANCE FROM EMOTION?
NO, BRUCE-KUN...
...THE AIM OF MEDITATION IS NOT TO ESCAPE FEELING.
THE AIM IS NOT TO PUSH EMOTION UNDER-GROUND.
YOU MEDITATE TO BEAR WITNESS TO YOUR EMOTIONS WITHOUT JUDGMENT.
ONLY BY KNOWING THEM CAN YOU AVOID SUCCUMBING TO THEM IN WAYS THAT MIGHT HURT YOU OR CAUSE HARM TO OTHERS.
DO NOT BLOCK OFF PARTS OF YOUR-SELF, BRUCE-KUN. WE ARE ALL HUMAN. WE ARE ALL MADE UP OF DARKNESS AND LIGHT.
LET YOURSELF BE FULL.

TUMMO MEDITATION IS AN ELEMENTAL BATTLE BETWEEN BLOOD AND ICE.
ICE. BLOOD. THEY WILL TEACH YOU EVERYTHING YOU NEED TO KNOW.
BUT FIRST, YOU MUST LEARN TO OVERRIDE YOUR BODY'S MOST BASIC INSTINCTS.
YOU SHUDDER AND CHATTER LIKE A CHILD, TRYING IN VAIN TO RAISE YOUR TEMPERATURE.
YOU ARE LETTING IT CONTROL YOU, LETTING IT DRIVE YOU INTO HYPOTHERMIA.
FIND TOTAL MUSCULAR RELAXATION. CIRCULATE HEAT TO THE SURFACE OF YOUR SKIN. THINK ON NOTHING BUT THIS.
YOUR FOCUS IS LAUGHABLE. WHAT ARE YOU THINKING OF?
I DON'T KNOW.
THIS GIRL.
A GIRL?
TO GRASP AFTER LOVE IS TO FEAR BEING ALONE IN THE FACE OF THE UNKNOWN. BUT THE UNKNOWN IS EVERY MINUTE OF EVERY DAY.
TO NEED OTHERS, BRUCE-KUN, IS TO FEAR LIFE ITSELF.
YOUR TASK IS TO NOT FEAR. TO NOT GRASP AFTER LOVE. TO EMBRACE BEING SEPARATE, APART.
IF YOU CARRY LOVE, YOU CARRY WEAKNESS.

MIO! SEE TO THE CUSTOMER. AND TRY NOT TO *TALK* HIM TO DEATH.
DON'T FORGET YOUR SLIP.
Meet me at the Botanical GARDens 12 Noon Tomorrow

WHAT ARE YOU THINKING OF?
MY PARENTS.
AFFECTION AND GRIEF ARE HUMAN. WHO YOU WISH TO BECOME WILL HAVE NO NEED FOR THEM.
THE DEATH OF YOUR PARENTS IS THE BEST THING THAT COULD HAVE HAPPENED TO YOU. IT FREED YOU FROM THE CONSTRAINTS OF MORTALITY.
YOU ARE DESTINED TO BE MORE THAN HUMAN...
...YOU ARE DESTINED TO SOAR LIKE A GOD.

I SEE A DINOSAUR.
I SEE A CAR.
A TENNIS RACKET.
A FRYING PAN.
A STRING OF PEARLS.
SUCH STRONG HANDS. AND POWERFUL FOREARMS.
AND YOUR *WATCH*...
...IT'S SO BEAUTIFUL.
CATCH ME IF YOU CAN!
DON'T TOUCH THAT, MIO! GIVE IT BACK, **NOW!**
IT WAS MY FATHER'S AND HE...AND MY MOTHER... THEY...
I SHOULDN'T DO THIS.

THIS REQUIRES COMPLETE MASTERY OF MIND. OF BODY. OF THE VERY BLOOD IN YOUR VEINS.
TOTAL FOCUS. TOTAL CONTROL.
YOU ARE GREATER THAN FLESH AND BONE. GREATER THAN ICE AND BLOOD, COLD AND HEAT, EARTH OR SKY.
YOU ARE INDOMITABLE.
BRUCE-KUN!
NOW, BRUCE-KUN. NOW I AM PROUD.

HE LOCKS THE DOORS.
HE LOCKS HIMSELF IN HERE, EVERY NIGHT. LIKE SOME RARE JEWEL.
HE IS ONE OF THE WORLD'S GREATEST ZEN WARRIORS.
HE AMASSED ONE OF THE LARGEST FORTUNES IN JAPAN AND TRANSPORTED IT HERE. WEALTH AND STRENGTH BEYOND THE IMAGINATION...
...BUT AT WHAT COST?
HIS FORTUNE, HIS DISCIPLINE, IT HAS HARDENED HIM. TURNED HIM COLD.
HIS HEART IS STONE. OUR HOUSE, LIKE A MAUSOLEUM.
BUT YOU, BRUCE-KUN...
...YOU STILL HAVE A CHANCE TO NOT BE THIS.
A CHANCE AT ANOTHER LIFE. A RICH LIFE, FULL OF LOVE AND WARMTH.
I KNOW WHAT HAPPENED TO YOUR PARENTS...BUT YOU STILL HAVE A KIND HEART. DO NOT OVER-PROTECT IT AND LET IT WITHER.
SHARE IT WITH SOMEONE ELSE.
IT'S NOT TOO LATE FOR YOU, MY SON.

KR-KRAK
TPTP
BRUCE! YOU'LL CATCH YOUR DEATH OUT THERE!
I DON'T CARE. I HAD TO SEE YOU, MIO. I HAD TO TELL YOU THAT I'M SORRY.
AND I DO WANT TO SEE YOU, SEE MORE OF YOU, IF THAT'S OKAY. AND--AND--
YOU MUST GO. MY FATHER, IF HE AWAKENS AND YOU ARE HERE, IT WILL BE BAD FOR ME.
THEN YOU COME TO ME. I WILL LEAVE A WINDOW OPEN BY THE BONSAI GARDEN.
I WILL. I WILL COME TONIGHT.
I PROMISE. NOW GO.

HAI!
BRUCE-KUN!
EEYAA!

UFF!
MIO?!
WHY?
...PLANNED EVERY...PAID ME...
WHO?

WHHHP
YOU WANTED...MY FORTUNE?
YES.
AND... COULD NO LONGER...LIVE IN THIS TOMB WITH YOU.
...BRUCE-KUN... LET THIS BE...YOUR FINAL LESSON...WRIT IN BLOOD AND ICE...

"...THIS IS WHAT CLOSENESS WILL BRING YOU."

Written by GREGG HURWITZ Pencilled by TONY S. DANIEL
Inks by RICHARD FRIEND Additional art by PERE PEREZ
colors by TOMEU MOREY lettering by JARED K. FLETCHER
cover by DANIEL, FRIEND, and MOREY

WAYNE MAN
SEVEN YEARS AGO...
A terrible idea flashes through my mind **every** time the doorbell rings.
DING DONG
An idea that would change everything that my life has become after all these years alone in Wayne Manor.
I've never stopped believing that Bruce is still out there.
No matter how long it has been since I've heard his voice, I know in my heart that I'll hear it again.
But the rational side of my brain always counters that belief in moments like this... offering an idea that could be **closer** to the truth.
DIIIIING DONG
That one of these days that door will open and I'll hear that my boy has died somewhere on the other end of the world.
That lurking **fear** tends to blind me from another horrible truth...
THE LONG WAIT
JAMES TYNION IV-WRITER
HENRIK JONSSON-PENCILS
SANDU FLOREA-INKS
JOHN KALISZ-COLORS DEZI SIENTY-LETTERS

...that there are those in this city who *hope* he is dead as much as I believe that he's *still* out there, alive.
MR. PENNYWORTH! I WAS STARTING TO GET WORRIED.
OF COURSE YOU WERE, MR. SHAW. AND WHAT HAVE YOU COME TO PESTER ME ABOUT TODAY?
C'MON NOW, AL. WE'VE BEEN PLAYING THIS GAME FOR TOO LONG TO MAKE IT *PERSONAL.*
I AGREE WITH YOU, MR. SHAW. WE CERTAINLY HAVE BEEN DOING THIS FOR *QUITE* SOME TIME.
LONG ENOUGH FOR YOU AND YOUR EMPLOYERS TO KNOW WHERE I STAND. I BELIEVE I MADE IT CLEAR YOU WEREN'T TO APPROACH ME ABOUT THIS MATTER AGAIN.
LOOK, WITH THE DEATH OF HER SON AND ONLY HEIR, THE KANE FAMILY HAS A *LEGAL RIGHT* TO MARTHA WAYNE'S FORTUNE AND PROPERTY.
FORGIVE ME IF I MISSED SOMETHING, MR. SHAW--
--BUT WHERE IS THIS NEW EVIDENCE THAT *BRUCE WAYNE* IS DEAD?

HE HASN'T BEEN SEEN OR HEARD FROM IN *YEARS!*
HOW MANY PRIVATE INVESTIGATORS HAVE YOU HIRED? HOW MUCH OF THE WAYNE FORTUNE HAVE YOU FUNNELED INTO TRYING TO FIND HIM?
AND WHAT HAS IT GOTTEN YOU?
...THERE WERE RUMORS HE WAS SPOTTED A YEAR AGO IN THE FOOT-HILLS OF THE HIMALAYAS.
RUMORS, HOPE, AND HEARSAY. THAT'S ALL YOU HAVE.
NO, MR. SHAW, I HAVE A GREAT DEAL *MORE* THAN THAT.
BY A BINDING LEGAL COMPACT IN THE WILLS OF THOMAS AND MARTHA WAYNE, I AM THE *SOLE* CUSTODIAN OF WAYNE MANOR AND THE WAYNE FORTUNE UNTIL SUCH TIME AS THEIR SON CLAIMS IT FOR HIMSELF.
DO YOU KNOW *WHY*, MR. SHAW? IT ISN'T THAT MRS. WAYNE LACKED RELATIVES IN THIS CITY, AS YOU ARE WELL AWARE.
SHE KNEW *PRECISELY* THE KIND OF MEN HER FATHER AND BROTHERS WERE.
AND SHE *REFUSED* TO LET EVERYTHING SHE SPENT HER LIFE BUILDING FALL INTO *THEIR HANDS.*

WELL, SHE'S NOT HERE, NOW, IS SHE? IT'S JUST YOU AND ME AND THE CONSIDERABLE RESOURCES I HAVE AT MY BACK.
MR. KANE IS PREPARED TO BE VERY GENEROUS. WE'LL MAKE YOU INDEPENDENTLY WEALTHY. ALL YOU HAVE TO DO IS SIGN THIS MANSION AWAY...
...YOU DON'T WANT TO BE LOCKED UP IN THIS OLD, ROTTING CAVE FOREVER, DO YOU?
NO, ALFRED...YOU WANT TO ACT. I'VE SEEN THE PLAYBILLS FROM LONDON.
HOW LONG HAS IT BEEN SINCE YOU'VE FELT THOSE STAGE LIGHTS ON YOUR FACE? THE ROAR OF THE CROWDS...
HELL, MR. KANE PUTS IN A CALL TO THE GOTHAM SHAKESPEARE COMPANY AND YOU'RE THE STAR IN THEIR NEXT BIG SHOW.
YOU KNOW MR. KANE...HE'S A TREMENDOUS SUPPORTER OF THE ARTS.
AND IF YOU DON'T SIGN? WE'LL STRIP EVERY DIME FROM YOUR POCKET AND LEAVE YOU TO STARVE ON THE STREETS.
DO YOU UNDERSTAND ME, ALFRED? WE'LL DESTROY YOU.
YOU CAN DAMN WELL TRY!
NOW GET THE HELL OUT OF THIS HOUSE BEFORE YOU SEE PRECISELY HOW DISAGREEABLE I AM PREPARED TO GET, MR. SHAW.

SLAM
DIING
WHAT NOW?! DID YOU FORGET TO THREATEN MY ROSE GARDEN WHILE YOU WERE AT IT?!

I CAN'T SAY THAT WAS MY EXACT INTENTION.
IT'S GOOD TO SEE YOU AGAIN, ALFRED.

MASTER BRUCE? IS IT REALLY YOU?
IT'S REALLY ME.
I'VE MISSED YOU, TOO, OLD FRIEND.
I'VE MISSED YOU, TOO.
WHO WAS THAT MAN, JUST THEN? HE SHOT OUT OF HERE LIKE A BAT OUT OF HELL...
IT DOESN'T MATTER, SIR. NOT ANYMORE.
AND FRANKLY, AFTER YOUR PARTICU-LARLY HARROWING BRAND OF TOURISM, I DON'T THINK YOU'RE THE ONE WHO GETS TO ASK QUESTIONS JUST YET.
I'M GOING TO TELL YOU EVERYTHING, ALFRED, BUT I ASSURE YOU...I WAS DOING QUITE A BIT MORE THAN TOURING ALL THESE YEARS.
I'VE BEEN TRAINING.

TRAINING...? FOR WHAT?
EVERYTHING, ALFRED. EVERYTHING I COULD POSSIBLY THINK OF. AND MORE.
I KNOW THE LAST FEW YEARS MUST HAVE BEEN HORRIBLE FOR YOU. NOT KNOWING IF I WAS ALIVE OR DEAD.
BUT I COULDN'T LET ANYONE SEE WHAT I WAS BUILDING MYSELF INTO. I COULDN'T LET THEM SEE WHAT I'VE STARTED TO PLAN.
I KNOW THAT YOU MIGHT FIND IT HARD TO FORGIVE...
...YOU NEVER STOPPED BELIEVING IN ME, ALFRED... DID YOU?
NOT FOR AN INSTANT, MASTER BRUCE.
I KNEW I COULD ALWAYS COUNT ON YOU...
SIT DOWN, OLD FRIEND. I'VE GOT A LONG STORY TO TELL YOU...AND AN IDEA.
AN IDEA THAT COULD CHANGE EVERYTHING.

GOTHAM'S EAST END...
Nailed me.
I...geez... shoulda known the score.
Soon as it turned upside down on me.
I get it now. I get what they did.
But...grhhn! It's too damn late.
I'm a dead man.
BAM BAM BAM
PASSWORD?
IT'S...IT'S BETTER... TO...
...TO TRAVEL WELL...THEN TO ARRIVE... UGHNNN
JUST OPEN THE DAMN DOOR, VINNIE!

MR. DENT?!

TWO-FACE IN: WELCOME TO THE DARK SIDE
WRITTEN BY TONY S. DANIEL
ART BY SZYMON KUDRANSKI
COLORS BY JOHN KALISZ LETTERS BY DEZI SIENTY
MR. DENT, WHAT HAPPENED?
WHAT DOES IT LOOK LIKE?
I THINK YOUR ROAD TO ENLIGHTENMENT TOOK A DETOUR.

PURIFY THE IMPURE WOUNDS OF MR. DENT SO NO FOREIGN ELEMENTS CAN TAINT THEM.
CLEAN AND SEW UP THE WOUND.
I WILL TEND TO THE MOST CORRUPT PORTION.
HIS *MIND.*

THIRTEEN DAYS AGO...
I BELIEVE IN GOOD AND EVIL, HARDEN.
I MEAN... THAT'S A COMMON CONCEPT MOST PEOPLE CARRY WITH THEM.
YOU LOOK LIKE A SMART GUY...I IMAGINE YOU HAVE SIMILAR BELIEFS, TOO.
EVEN THE HOLIEST OF SAINTS IS CAPABLE OF COMMITTING THE MOST HORRIFIC OF SINS... IF THEY'RE PUT IN THE RIGHT--
--OR WRONG SITUATION.
LISTEN, HARDEN. I'M NOT A MIND READER. I HAVE NO IDEA IF YOU'RE LYING TO ME.
SPNT
IT'S ALL UP TO THE FLIP OF THE COIN, FAR AS I'M CONCERNED.
M-MY GOD, DENT...WH-WHAT SIDE DID THE COIN LAND ON?!

YOU DON'T WANT TO KNOW. TRUST ME.
IT'S THE TRUTH! THE PROSECUTOR IS DROPPING ALL CHARGES! TH-TH-THE EVIDENCE WAS CONTAMINATED--JUST AS YOUR ATTORNEYS SAID!
DON'T YOU SEE? I-I'M JUST RELAYING THE GOOD NEWS!
THEN IT'S SETTLED, RIGHT? IF I'M OFF THE HOOK, IF THERE'S NO EVIDENCE, I SHOULD GET BACK MY JOB AS THE D.A. OF GOTHAM.
LISTEN, THAT'S THE THING. IT'S JUST--HE WANTS A MEETING FIRST. THE PROSECUTOR, MR. DOMINIC STERANO, THAT IS.
A MEETING? DOMINIC NEVER CARED MUCH FOR OL' HARVEY DENT. EVEN TRIED BEDDING MY EX-WIFE ONCE.
HE'S BEEN LEADIN' THE CRUSADE AGAINST ME EVER SINCE I WAS A YOUNG, GOOD LOOKING DISTRICT ATTORNEY. YOU SEE HOW I THINK THIS DOESN'T SMELL RIGHT?

'SIDES ALL THAT, WHY'D HE SEND YOU BY YOUR LONESOME, PACKING HEAT?
I HAVE A CONCEAL-TO-CARRY LICENSE. THIS IS GOTHAM CITY, DENT! YOU CAN UNDERST--
SHUT YOUR FACE!
WHY DIDN'T HE CALL ME HIMSELF? MY LAWYER IS RIGHT HERE. DOMINIC HASN'T CALLED YOU, McMURPHY, HAS HE?
NOT A ONCE, MR. DENT.
THMP
THIS DOESN'T LOOK GOOD FOR YOU, HARDEN.
URRGH!
CALL STERANO'S OFFICE! I SWEAR HE SENT ME! IT'S THE TRUTH!
WE ALREADY DID. SEEMS HE'S BEEN CONVENIENTLY OUT OF TOWN. TSK TSK.
WE'LL GET TO THE BOTTOM OF THIS, HARDEN. IT MIGHT TAKE US ALL NIGHT, BUT WE WILL.
BOYS? LET'S SHOW OUR GUEST THE PLAYROOM.
N-NO! YOU'RE MAKING A MISTAKE!

YAAAARGGHHH
HE'S WORKING FOR SOMEONE, McMURPHY. AND I DON'T THINK IT'S JUST THE PROSECUTOR.
THEY KNOW THEIR CASE WILL BE DROPPED BY THE JUDGE EVENTUALLY, HARVEY.
I THINK ALL THESE BLOWN CASES HAVE MADE YOU A SEVERE DETRIMENT TO THE PROSECUTOR'S AMBITIONS.
I DON'T BUY THAT DOMINIC STERANO IS LOOKING TO BUMP ME OFF. NOT IN HIS CHARACTER. THERE'S SOMEONE ELSE WHO HAS SOMETHING TO GAIN. HAS TO BE.
HE'S HELD UP FOR ALMOST TWO HOURS UNDER THAT BLOW-TORCH.
BEEP DEE-DEEP
McMURPHY, IF THERE'S ONE THING I'VE LEARNED, IT'S THE ONES WITH THE MOST TO LOSE WHO HOLD OUT THE LONGEST.
YARGHH-
-YARGHH-
WELL? WHO IS IT?
--YAAAAGH
THE PROSECUTOR'S OFFICE. THEY DID SEND HARDEN AFTER ALL. DOMINIC WANTS TO SET UP A MEETING FOR TOMORROW AFTER-NOON.
CUT THE HEAT AND BANDAGE HIM UP, LOUIS. AND DROP HIM OFF AT THE E.R....TONIGHT'S HIS LUCKY NIGHT.
S-SERIOUSLY? SO...THE COIN...WAS IT...?
THE GOOD SIDE, HARDEN. WHAT ELSE?

GOTHAM CITY'S LOWER EAST END...
Dominic Sterano.
Gotham's Golden Boy of the Law. State Prosecutor. And these last coupl'a years, a major thorn in my side.
But he's not foolin' me. He's been after my hide since I was district attorney, and I've been his pet project ever since my...accident.
But nothin' his department tried to pin on me has stuck, which doesn't make him look too good.
I admit, I'm no angel.
But some of the things he's tried to pin on me are complete bull spit.
Except this last one. There might be some truth to it. I can't oversee all of my business partners. If someone was to get arrested...
...well, they might point a finger in my direction to save their own skin.
But I got friends. Good friends in high places that owe me big.
HARVEY, THANKS FOR AGREEING TO MEET ME. WE NEED TO TALK.
DAMN RIGHT WE DO, STERANO. SO SPILL IT.
And whether Dominic knows that or not, there's a fifty-fifty chance I'm walkin' away from anything he can throw at me.
He doesn't like them odds, so he's probably lookin' to cut some sort of deal here.
TWO FACE IN: 50/50
WRITTEN BY TONY S. DANIEL
ART BY SZYMON KUDRANSKI
COLORS BY JOHN KALISZ
LETTERS BY DEZI SIENTY

WE'VE BEEN PLAYING THIS CAT AND MOUSE GAME FOR TOO LONG.
TO BE HONEST, I'M GETTING SICK OF THE CHASE. YOU'VE WON, HARVEY. I'M CALLING OFF MY HOUNDS.
HOW'D YOU LIKE YOUR OLD JOB BACK, AS GOTHAM CITY'S D.A.?
JUST LIKE THAT, EH? I LOOK STUPID TO YOU, DOMINIC?
BOYS...
HEY--YOU WERE SUPPOSED TO BE ALONE, HARV!
AGAIN, DO I LOOK STUPID TO YOU?
NO WIRE. HE'S GOOD, BOSS.
SO, EVEN IF I CAN GET REINSTATED--
YOU CAN. AND YOU WILL. I'LL PULL THE PROPER STRINGS.
NEW EVIDENCE CAN POSSIBLY BE BROUGHT TO LIGHT THAT JUDGE ALBRIGHT HAS BEEN IN ON THE TAKE--
--WITH THE SOLE JOB OF BRINGING YOU DOWN. HECK, WE CAN POSSIBLY EVEN CONNECT HIM TO YOUR, WELL...YOUR CONDITION.
YOU SAID POSSIBLY. WHAT'S THE CATCH?
THIS LADY IN THE PIC WITH ME... SHE'S NOT MY WIFE. BUT, SHE'S MY... FRIEND.
SOMEONE YOU AND I KNOW IS TRYING TO BLACKMAIL ME. HARVEY, YOU'RE THE ONLY ONE I CAN GO TO FOR SOMETHING LIKE THIS.
I'M SCREWED HERE. ROYALLY SCREWED.
WHY SHOULD I RISK MY NECK? SEEMS ONE WAY OR ANOTHER, YOU'RE GOING DOWN.
I HAVE YOU WHETHER YOU KNOW IT OR NOT. I HAVE EVIDENCE AND WITNESSES READY SO YOU'LL NEVER GAIN YOUR CREDIBILITY OR YOUR OLD JOB. YOU'LL NEVER SEE THE LIGHT OF DAY.
THEN WE'LL BOTH BE GOING DOWN.
OR...WE CAN HELP EACH OTHER. IT'S YOUR CALL, HARVEY.
WHO HAS HER?

"FREAKSHOW TOMMY. YOU KNOW WHER--"
SAND TAVERN
"YEAH. YEAH, I KNOW FREAKSHOW. I KNOW HIM WELL.
"SO WHAT DO YOU WANT ME TO DO?"
"WHATEVER YOU HAVE TO."
WHERE'S MAURICE, SWEETHEART?
THIS IS A PRIVATE PARTY, UGLY.
SWEETHEART SAYS GET YOUR UGLY MUG OUTTA HERE 'FORE I RIP YOUR HEAD OFF AND ROLL IT OUT.
I'M SORRY, WHAT DID YOU SAY? CHARLIE, CAN YOU TRANSLATE IDIOT-SPEAK FOR ME?
I CAN'T HEAR HIM. HIS MOUTH IS FULL OF TABLE.
CRAAASSSSH
BLAM BLAM
PARTY'S OVER! BOYS, TAKE YER UGLIES HOME AND DON'T FORGET THE PAPER BAGS.
NO ONE'S LEAVING 'CEPT YOU, UGLY. OR DO YOU CARE TO TRY THAT WITH ME?
SWEETHEART, THAT'S NOT HOW WE TREAT FAMILY! MI CASA, HIS CASA. EMPTY THE BAR AND BUY HIS FRIENDS A ROUND ON THE HOUSE, WILL YA?
LET ME AND THE BIG DOG... CATCH UP.
YEAH. FINE, MAURICE.

I'M NOT GONNA HURT YOU, MAURICE. ALL THAT OLD STUFF IS WATER UNDER THE BRIDGE.
YOU'RE A GOOD MAN. I ALWAYS SAID THAT--
I'M LOOKIN' FOR YOUR OLD FRIEND FREAK-SHOW. I NEED TO FIND HIM... TONIGHT.
AH, MAN. FREAKSHOW'S GOTTEN A LOT WORSE SINCE YOU LAST SAW HIM. HE DON'T EVEN WANNA BE SEEN.
NO LIE, NOBODY KNOWS WHERE'S HE'S HIDIN--
EXCEPT YOU...
CRASH
THEN GIMME SOME LUCKY GUESSES, DAMMIT.
I DON'T KNOW JACK. HE SENDS A SCRAWNY LITTLE RAGDOLL TO COME DOWN AND COLLECT NOWADAYS.
IF I KNEW WHERE HE WAS, I'D TELL YA--
WHERE'D THAT BAD LITTLE LADY GO? SHE SHOULD JOIN US FOR AN OLD FASHIONED.
MAYBE YOUR UGLY HORSE-FACE SCARED HER OFF. GO FIND HER.
UH, CHARLIE... THIS AIN'T GOOD!

DOUGIE? WHAT'S TAKIN' YOU SO LONG BACK THERE?
DOUGIE? AH, CRAP.
THUD THUD THUD
I'LL TELL YOU WHERE HE IS! CHILL OUT, MAN. BUT I SWEAR, IF HE FINDS OUT I TOLD YA HE'LL KILL ME. HE'LL UP AND KILL ME, YA HEAR?!
HE WON'T TOUCH YOU, 'CAUSE HE'LL BE DEAD.
BLAM BLAM BLAM BLAM BLAM
THE HELL'S GOING ON OUT THERE? YOU PULLIN' SOME-THING ON ME, MAURICE?

CHARLIE? DOUGIE? WHAT'S THE--
--MAURICE? YOU'D BETTER--
CRASH
Just what I need.
MAURICE?!

That little rat warns Freakshow I'm comin' and he'll have half the town lookin' for me.
Every gang this side of Crime Alley pays in to Freakshow. And for good reason.
While I've been distracted with building my defense against Sterano, Freakshow's been taking over like a fast-moving **staph infection.**
He's eaten up most of my associates' businesses, grown his weapons cache, and built alliances with my enemies using a lot of what should've been **my** capital.
Whether Dominic Sterano knew it or not, Freakshow was already on my radar.
It was just a matter of time before I found him in my crosshairs...
...or I ended up in his.
WHAT IN HOLY HELL, MAURICE?
HARVEY DENT--

--YOU HAVE BEEN CHOSEN BY OUR LEADER.
CHOSEN? FOR WHAT?
THOOP
RUN AND INFORM THE LEADER. WE HAVE SUCCEEDED.

HE LOOKS FAR WORSE THAN DESCRIBED, LEADER.
LOOKS CAN BE *DECEIVING,* YOUNG PUPIL. I TAUGHT YOU THAT IN WEEK ONE.
WAKE HIM UP, PLEASE.
TWO FACE IN:
THE BIG FALL
WRITTEN BY TONY S. DANIEL
ART BY SZYMON KUDRANSKI
COLORS BY JOHN KALISZ
LETTERS BY DEZI SIENTY

OF COURSE, LEADER.
SPLOOSH
HARGH!
I HAVE MUCH WORK TO DO HERE, MR. DENT.
RIDDING THE WORLD OF EVIL ONE PERSON AT A TIME TAKES A CERTAIN AMOUNT OF TENACITY.
WHO THE HELL ARE YOU?
I COULD BE YOUR SAVIOR OR YOUR EXECU-TIONER. IT'S UP TO YOU TO DECIDE.
THE COIN WAS FLIPPED FOR YOU LONG AGO...AND I AM STILL BLIND TO ITS ANSWER.
YOU TOOK MY COIN?! I'LL DESTROY YOU, BALDILOCKS! I'LL LITERALLY TEAR YOU A NEW--
SILENCE. YOU DO NOT NEED TO BE FULLY ENLIGHTENED FOR THIS DUTY OF MINE...YET.
TWNK
...
I FEAR FOR THIS ONE.
SO MUCH ANGER. HATRED. FEAR. IT'S CAPSIZING HIS WHOLE BEING.
HE WILL NOT LIVE LONG ENOUGH FOR ME TO ATTEMPT PURIFICATION.

I SEEK ANSWERS TO YOUR DARKNESS, HARVEY DENT. I'VE RELEASED THE VALVE OF A HIGHLY PRESSURIZED STORM.
FEAR NOT FOR YOU, BUT FOR ME. FOR MY MIND IS PURE AND ABOUT TO BE FLOODED WITH...
...
?!
IS IT THE DARKNESS WITHIN HIM THAT'S MOVED YOU, LEADER?
NO, PUPIL...
...IT WAS THE LIGHT.

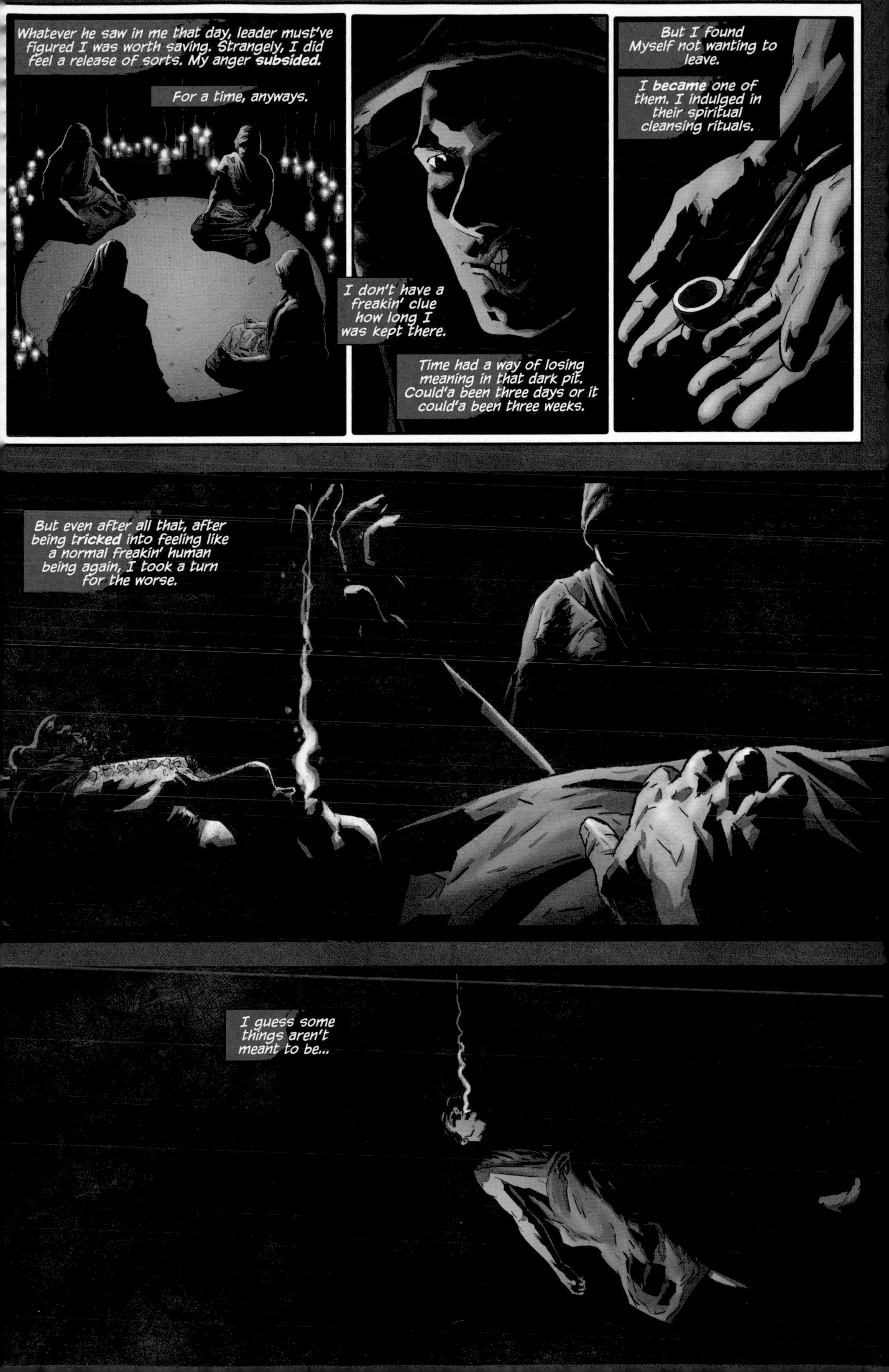
Whatever he saw in me that day, leader must've figured I was worth saving. Strangely, I did feel a release of sorts. My anger subsided.
For a time, anyways.
I don't have a freakin' clue how long I was kept there.
Time had a way of losing meaning in that dark pit. Could'a been three days or it could'a been three weeks.
But I found Myself not wanting to leave.
I became one of them. I indulged in their spiritual cleansing rituals.
But even after all that, after being tricked into feeling like a normal freakin' human being again, I took a turn for the worse.
I guess some things aren't meant to be...

WAKE HIM UP, PUPIL.
HARGH! YA KNOW, LEADER, THERE ARE BETTER WAYS OF WAKIN' A MAN UP...
SPLOOSH
IT'S ONCE AGAIN TIME FOR ME TO ENTER YOUR MIND, HARVEY DENT. NOW THAT WE HAVE A BOND, YOU WILL NOT BE AS AVERSE TO MY VIOLATION.

I'M SORRY.
I CANNOT HELP YOU.
YOU MUST GO. GO AND FIGHT YOUR DEMONS YOUR OWN WAY.
MY OWN WAY? WHAT ARE YOU SAYING, CHIEF?
YOU WILL FIND YOUR COIN IN YOUR COAT POCKET, WHERE IT BELONGS. I CANNOT HELP YOU ANY FURTHER.
But leader *would* still help me.

GOTHAM'S EDGEWATER DISTRICT.
TWO-FACE HASN'T BEEN SEEN FOR ALMOST A WEEK, TOMMY. I LOST CONTACT WITH HIM WHEN MAURICE BIT IT.
I THINK IT'S SAFE FOR YOU TO START THINKING OF TAKING OVER HIS SHIPPING PORTS.
COLOR ME UNCONVINCED, STERANO. THERE'S NO PROOF TWO-FACE IS DEAD.
THEY WERE YOUR HIRE, FREAKSHOW--SORRY, TOMMY. YOU HIRED THEM.
THE ONE CONDITION LEADER HAD WAS THAT HE WOULDN'T KILL ANYONE WHO WAS STILL CAPABLE OF GOOD. HE WAS PARTICULAR ABOUT ROOTING OUT ONLY PEOPLE "INFESTED WITH DARKNESS."
I DON'T KNOW WHERE THEY'RE HIDING OUT. BUT IF TWO-FACE IS STILL ALIVE, I'LL HAVE A FULL-SCALE GANG WAR ON MY HANDS.
THINGS ARE TOO FRAGILE THESE DAYS. ESPECIALLY WITH THE UNCERTAINTY SURROUNDING CITY HALL AFTER THAT COUNCILMAN WAS DECAPITATED IN MAYOR HADY'S OFFICE.
DON'T WORRY ABOUT TWO-FACE. MY BOYS HAVE MADE THE ROUNDS AND INFORMED HIS ASSOCIATES THAT THEIR BOSS IS FINISHED.
IF HE IS ALIVE, HE'LL FIND HIMSELF ONE LONE WOLF WHEN HE COMES OUT OF HIDING.
FLK
AND YOU'LL TAKE CARE OF THAT LONE WOLF YOURSELF THEN, EH, STERANO? WELL, I SAY WE SIT TIGHT AND MAKE SURE. I DIDN'T GET TO THIS POINT BY RUSHING THINGS.
BUT WE'RE IN A RUSH! WE HAVE SHIPMENTS COMING IN TONIGHT. THEY'RE ALL YOURS.
AND BY YOURS, MY BABY MEANS OURS.
LYDIA, BABE, YOU SHOULD'A STAYED IN THE CAR. I TOLD YOU I'D ONLY BE A MINUTE. HOW COME MY BODYGUARDS DIDN'T STOP YOU?
BODYGUARDS? I DIDN'T SEE ANY--

BAM
AH!
DON'T WORRY ABOUT YER BODY-GUARDS, STERANO. I GAVE 'EM THE NIGHT OFF.

GOTHAM CITY'S EDGEWATER DISTRICT...
ONE THING ABOUT A "LONE WOLF," STERANO-- THEY DON'T RELY ON OTHERS FOR THEIR OWN SURVIVAL.
HARV-- HARVEY! LISTEN UP, PAL. THIS IS A HUGE MISTAKE!
SHUT UP, STERANO. GIVE TWO-FACE SOME RESPECT.
WHO D'YA THINK WE'RE DEALIN' WITH, HERE? SOME SCRUB?
WE'RE CAUGHT RED-HANDED.
THE BEST THING WE CAN DO IS MAKE A SUITABLE AGREEMENT THE THREE OF US CAN BE SATISFIED WITH.
CHA-CLAK
I'LL GIVE YOU MY PROPOSITION FIRST.

BRAKA
BRAKABRAKA

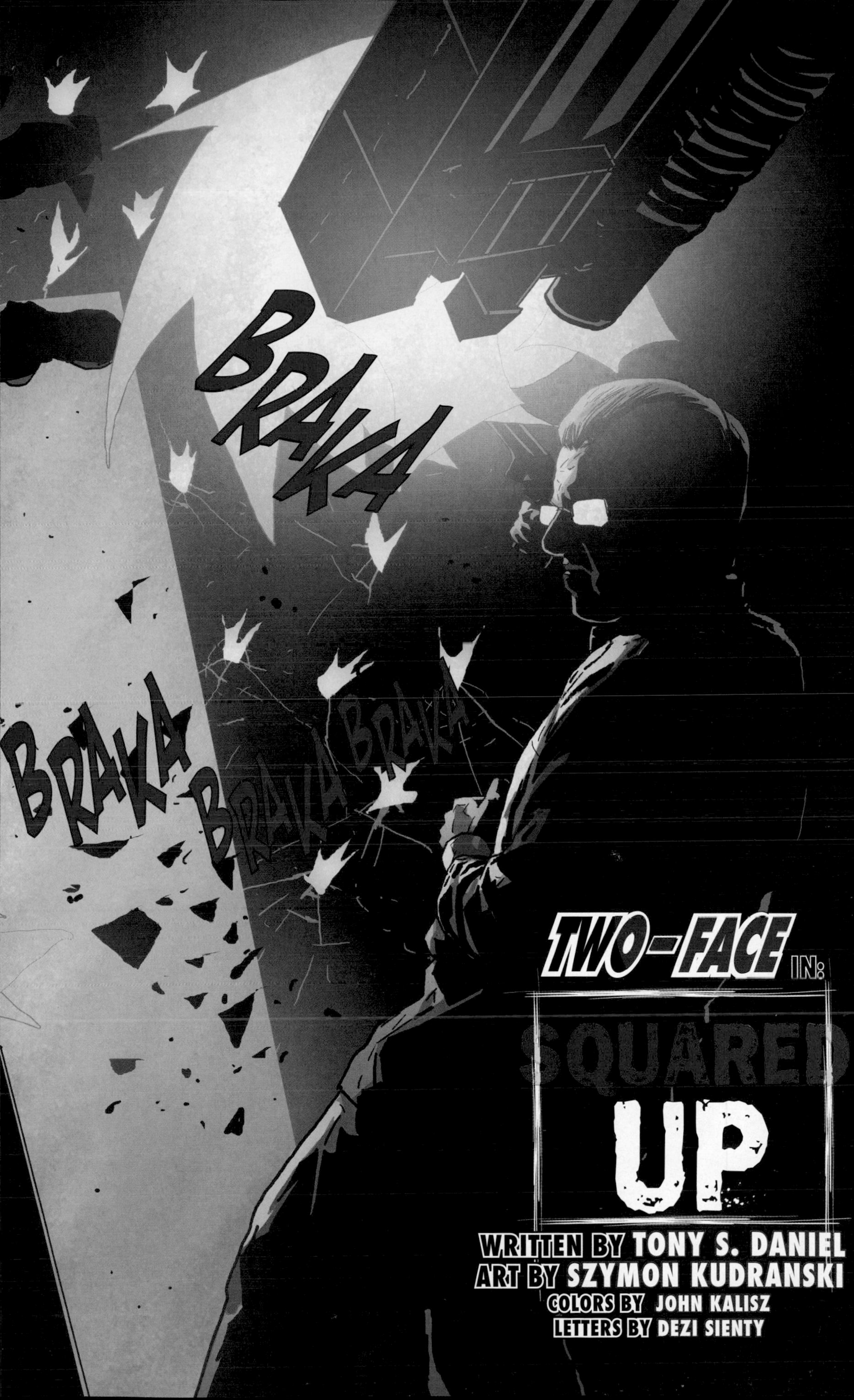

BRAKA
BRAKA
BRAKA
BRAKA
BRAKA
TWO-FACE IN:
SQUARED UP
WRITTEN BY TONY S. DANIEL
ART BY SZYMON KUDRANSKI
COLORS BY JOHN KALISZ
LETTERS BY DEZI SIENTY

BLAM!
GGARGGHH! YOU--YOU KILLED HIM!
YOU'RE UNDER CITIZEN'S ARREST, HARVEY! PUT THE GUN DOWN!
ME? UNDER ARREST? YOU DON'T HAVE THE AUTHORITY.
BLAM BLAM
BLAM BLAM
CLK CLK CLK
GNN.
YOU'RE CRAZY!

HELP! SOMEONE--CALL THE POLICE!
BLAM
BLAM
BLAM
BLAM
CRASH
YOU KILLED MY BROTHER. YOU...YOU...
SERVES YOU BOTH RIGHT, FREAKSHOW.
THUD
I NEVER LIKED THAT JERK. THIS AIN'T THE FIRST TIME HE TRIED TO KILL ME.
HE WAS A SAINT!
I DON'T DECIDE WHERE YOU TWO WILL GO. I JUST PUNCH THE TICKET.
BLAM
BLAM
BLAM
BLAM

NOW.
OPEN THIS...
HE'S COME BACK, LEADER--WHAT SHALL WE DO WITH HIM?
WE SAVE HIS LIFE.
THERE IS NO OTHER CHOICE.

I don't remember how long I was lyin' there. Just awoke. Unable to move.
One thing I knew for sure...I was alive.
They freakin' saved me. Me!
Old kook couldn't bring himself to kill me after all.
His damned principles stopped him from doing what Freakshow Tommy and his sideshow brother hired him to do.
I HEARD EVERYTHING BEFORE I SHOT STERANO AND TOMMY. I UNDERSTAND YOU WERE HIRED TO KILL ME BUT DIDN'T HAVE THE GUTS.
THAT'S TWICE NOW, LEADER.
WHERE WOULD WE BE IF WE DID NOT HONOR OUR OWN VALUE, MR. DENT?
YOU SENT ME TO FREAKSHOW'S THINKING THEY WOULD TAKE ME OUT. YOU WERE WRONG.
I AM MERELY A HAPPENSTANCE IN YOUR LIFE. NO MORE, NO LESS. I WILL NOT AFFECT YOUR OUTCOME.
ONLY YOU CAN DO THAT.
WHEN ONE IS MADE OF EQUAL PARTS LIGHT AND DARK, ONE MUST MAKE A CHOICE. THAT CHOICE IS WHAT TIPS THE SCALE, MR. DENT.
I DON'T NEED YOU TO TELL ME THAT.

LOOKS LIKE YOUR LUCKY DAY.
BLAM
Pulling the trigger was the easy part. The coin is what tipped the scale.
I don't question which side the coin drops.
You either win or you lose.
You live or you die.
Or...
...You cheat.
END.

GOTHAM CITY POLICE DEPARTMENT...
GIVES "GRAVEYARD SHIFT" A WHOLE NEW MEANING, DON'T IT?
NOT THAT THE TERM'S EVER MEANT MUCH IN THIS CITY. ANY COP WORTH A DAMN HAS TO TAKE THE NIGHT SHIFT.
GOTHAM'S MONSTERS SLEEP IN THE DAYTIME, Y'KNOW?
BUT I GUESS YOU WOULDN'T. YOU'RE A TRANSFER.
NANCY, RIGHT?
GOT IT ON YOUR FIRST TRY, SGT. BULLOCK. THIS IS MY FIRST NIGHT.
HEH. FIGURED.
THEY'VE BEEN STICKING THE ROOKIES DOWN HERE FOR MONTHS. SEEING HOW LONG THEY LAST.
THE LAST GUY WE HAD WORKED IN THE EVIDENCE ROOM FOR EIGHT YEARS.
HE APPLIED FOR A TRANSFER JUST ONE NIGHT AFTER THAT SHOWED UP.
CAN'T SAY I BLAME HIM.

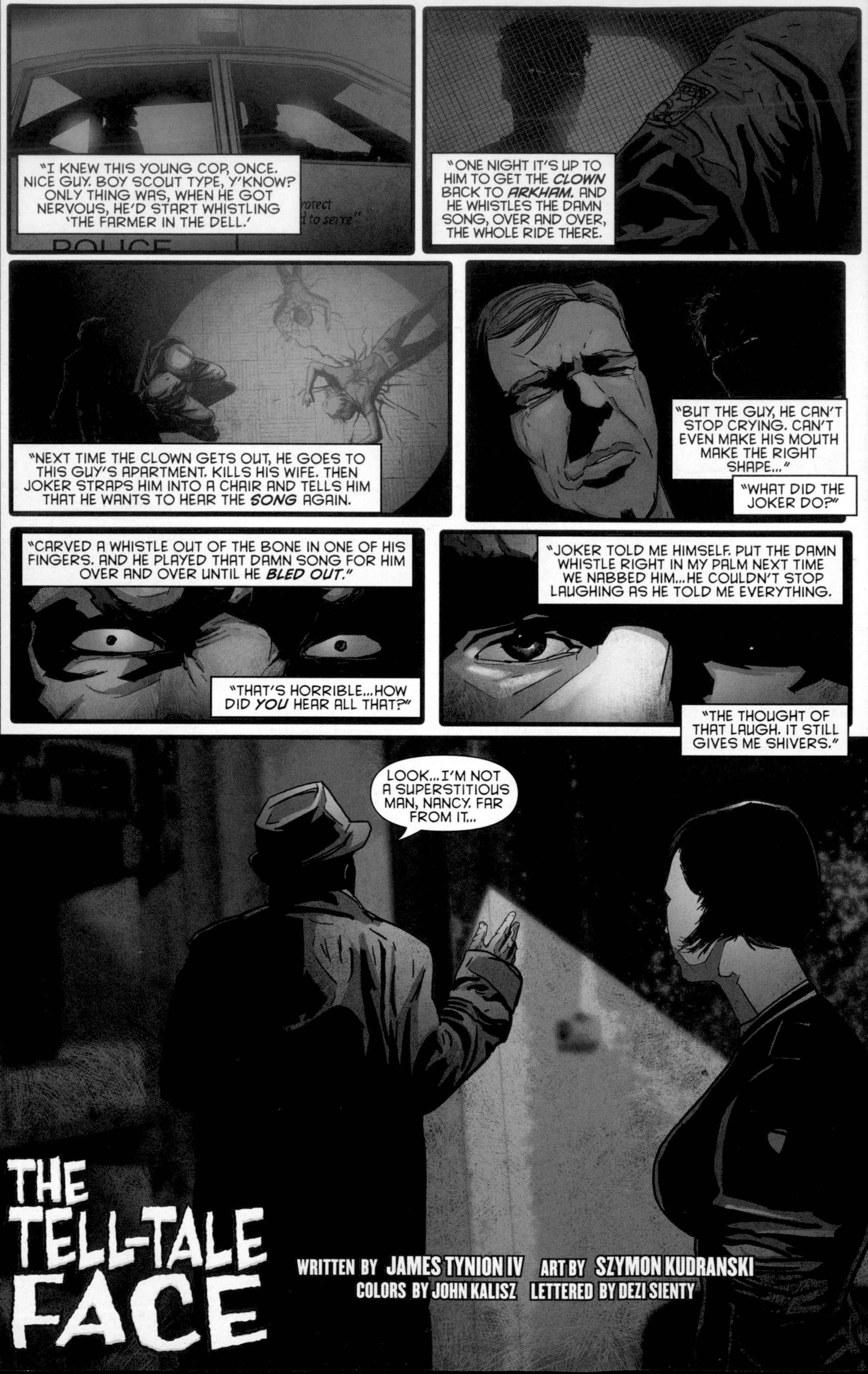
"I KNEW THIS YOUNG COP, ONCE. NICE GUY. BOY SCOUT TYPE, Y'KNOW? ONLY THING WAS, WHEN HE GOT NERVOUS, HE'D START WHISTLING 'THE FARMER IN THE DELL.'
"ONE NIGHT IT'S UP TO HIM TO GET THE CLOWN BACK TO ARKHAM. AND HE WHISTLES THE DAMN SONG, OVER AND OVER, THE WHOLE RIDE THERE.
"NEXT TIME THE CLOWN GETS OUT, HE GOES TO THIS GUY'S APARTMENT. KILLS HIS WIFE. THEN JOKER STRAPS HIM INTO A CHAIR AND TELLS HIM THAT HE WANTS TO HEAR THE SONG AGAIN.
"BUT THE GUY, HE CAN'T STOP CRYING. CAN'T EVEN MAKE HIS MOUTH MAKE THE RIGHT SHAPE..."
"WHAT DID THE JOKER DO?"
"CARVED A WHISTLE OUT OF THE BONE IN ONE OF HIS FINGERS. AND HE PLAYED THAT DAMN SONG FOR HIM OVER AND OVER UNTIL HE BLED OUT."
"THAT'S HORRIBLE...HOW DID YOU HEAR ALL THAT?"
"JOKER TOLD ME HIMSELF. PUT THE DAMN WHISTLE RIGHT IN MY PALM NEXT TIME WE NABBED HIM...HE COULDN'T STOP LAUGHING AS HE TOLD ME EVERYTHING.
"THE THOUGHT OF THAT LAUGH. IT STILL GIVES ME SHIVERS."
LOOK...I'M NOT A SUPERSTITIOUS MAN, NANCY. FAR FROM IT...
THE TELL-TALE FACE
WRITTEN BY JAMES TYNION IV ART BY SZYMON KUDRANSKI
COLORS BY JOHN KALISZ LETTERED BY DEZI SIENTY

"...BUT I'M SURE AS HELL GLAD IT'S NOT *ME* SITTING DOWN HERE ALONE WITH THAT THING FOR THE NEXT EIGHT HOURS."
HEH.

HELLO?
-SIGH- NOBODY'S IN HERE. IT'S JUST YOU, NANCY.
AAAA Ha HaHa Ha HAHAAA
AAAH!
6A2
5C2

SEE? NOTHING TO BE AFRAID OF, NANCY. JUST A *DEAD PILE OF SKIN.*
KLICK
A DEAD PILE OF SKIN THAT USED TO BE ATTACHED TO SOMEONE WHO HAS KILLED OVER *THREE HUNDRED PEOPLE* IN THE LAST FIVE YEARS.
WHAT'S SO SCARY ABOUT *THAT?*

HAAAA HA HAHA HA HAHAAA HA
AAAAAAAAAHHH! NO!
IT'S JUST IN YOUR HEAD, NANCY. IT'S JUST IN YOUR HEAD. PULL YOURSELF TOGETHER.
HUH?
THE HELL IS THAT?

BULLOCK!
HUH? NANCY? WHAT'RE *YOU* DOING UP HERE?
SMACK
YOU TAPED A DAMN AUDIO PLAYER TO THE BACK OF *THE JOKER'S FACE!* AFTER YOU TOLD ME THAT STORY...YOU *MONSTER!*
C'MON, I WAS JUST HAVING SOME *FUN.* YOU'RE A ROOKIE. THIS KINDA THING'S *MANDATORY.*
I'VE ONLY GOT RODRIGUEZ COVERING ME FOR FIVE MINUTES. BUT IF I GO BACK DOWN THERE AND THAT DAMN THING STARTS LAUGHING...I *WILL* REPORT YOU.
WON'T GIVE IT A SECOND THOUGHT. YOU *HEAR* ME?
I HEAR YA, I HEAR YA...
...*HEH.*
WELCOME TO THE FORCE, KID.

"YOU'RE GONNA FIT IN JUST FINE."
G.C.P.D
TIME TO PUT ON A HAPPY FACE!

Detective Comics #9 variant cover by Jason Fabok with Peter Steigerwald

ARKHAM
FABOK
2012

DC COMICS™

"A stunning debut. This is definitely in the top rank of the revamp."
—THE ONION / AV CLUB

"Snyder and Capullo reach new heights of collaboration here, with Capullo making inspired storytelling choices that add additional layers to Snyder's narration and dialog."
—VANITY FAIR

START AT THE BEGINNING!

BATMAN VOLUME 1: THE COURT OF OWLS

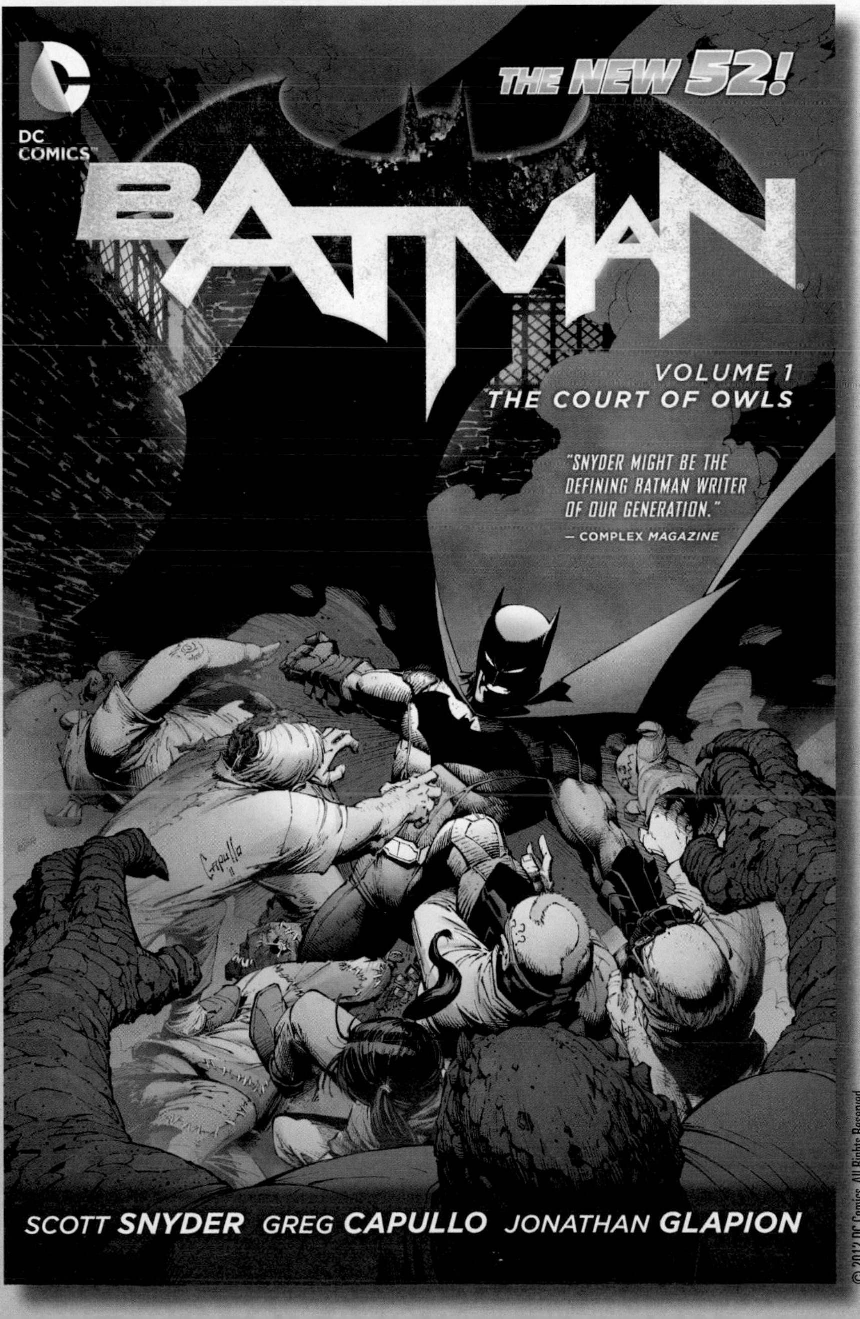

BATMAN & ROBIN VOLUME 1: BORN TO KILL

BATMAN: DETECTIVE COMICS VOLUME 1: FACES OF DEATH

BATMAN: THE DARK KNIGHT VOLUME 1: KNIGHT TERRORS

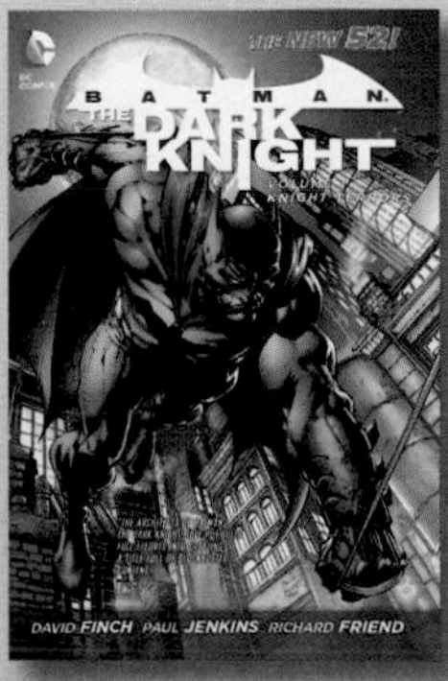